[美国] 斯特拉·Z. 特奥杜卢 拉维·K. 罗伊 著　付满 译

牛津通识读本·

公共管理
Public Administration
A Very Short Introduction

译林出版社

图书在版编目（CIP）数据

公共管理/（美）斯特拉·Z.特奥杜卢（Stella Z. Theodoulou），（美）拉维·K.罗伊（Ravi K. Roy）著；付满译. —南京：译林出版社，2023.10
（牛津通识读本）
书名原文：Public Administration: A Very Short Introduction
ISBN 978-7-5447-9851-8

I.①公⋯ II.①斯⋯ ②拉⋯ ③付⋯ III.①公共管理 IV.①D035-0

中国国家版本馆CIP数据核字（2023）第143581号

Public Administration: A Very Short Introduction, First Edition
by Stella Z. Theodoulou and Ravi K. Roy
Copyright © Stella Z. Theodoulou & Ravi K. Roy 2016
Public Administration was originally published in English in 2016. This licensed edition is published by arrangement with Oxford University Press. Yilin Press, Ltd is solely responsible for this bilingual edition from the original work and Oxford University Press shall have no liability for any errors, omissions or inaccuracies or ambiguities in such bilingual edition or for any losses caused by reliance thereon.
Chinese and English edition copyright © 2023 by Yilin Press, Ltd
All rights reserved.

著作权合同登记号　图字：10-2018-429号

公共管理　[美国]斯特拉·Z.特奥杜卢　拉维·K.罗伊／著　付满／译

责任编辑　陈　锐
装帧设计　景秋萍
校　　对　王　敏
责任印制　董　虎

原文出版　Oxford University Press, 2016
出版发行　译林出版社
地　　址　南京市湖南路1号A楼
邮　　箱　yilin@yilin.com
网　　址　www.yilin.com
市场热线　025-86633278
排　　版　南京展望文化发展有限公司
印　　刷　江苏凤凰通达印刷有限公司
开　　本　890毫米×1260毫米　1/32
印　　张　7.625
插　　页　4
版　　次　2023年10月第1版
印　　次　2023年10月第1次印刷
书　　号　ISBN 978-7-5447-9851-8
定　　价　39.00元

版权所有·侵权必究

译林版图书若有印装错误可向出版社调换　质量热线：025-83658316

序 言

孔繁斌

现代文明的形成和发展，逐步将政府的价值和作用呈现在公众面前，一个恪守公共利益、高效协同运作、卓越有效治理的政府，已经成为公众共同的期盼。正因为在当今文明治理中政府成为不可或缺的"大管家"和"总客服"，关于政府治理行动的知识体系既已成为现代社会的"通用知识"，无论是履行公共治理职责的管理者，还是公民个人、法人或其他社会主体，都参与到了政府治理行动知识的构建之中，并通过不断探索更加有效的知识管理，促进公共问题的解决和公共需求的满足。当然，这一领域的知识并非是零碎的经验性常识，而且与其他领域的知识一样，存在着分歧甚至争论。为此，近一百年以来，在当今社会科学发展中构建了专门探索政府治理价值和行动的公共行政学或公共管理学这样的知识体系，读者看到的这本《公共管理》即为对这一知识领域的核心知识予以简明呈现的通识读物。

作为牛津通识读本丛书的一种，本书向读者发出了进入公共管理世界的邀请，并在每章精巧设计了理论维度和国别探索相融合的叙述结构,对现代政府治理知识予以溯源与发展双重视角的描绘,生动概述了公共行政的起源与发展历程,同时也着眼当代公共行政分析的热点问题。尽管这本通识读物篇幅不长,但它不仅向读者敞开了公共管理之门,也让读者在初步接触公共管理学知识之际,能深刻感受到这门学科与人们的工作和生活是多么密切相关,或者说,现代政府治理知识体系的变化和发展,直接影响着人们美好生活梦想的实现。

作为以现代政府治理行动为主要研究对象的公共管理学,是伴随以工业化为主的现代文明兴起而逐步形成的,工业化深刻改变了社会结构和生活方式,涌现出大量复杂的公共问题,需要有政府这样的公共机构集中、高效地去解决。本书主要置于欧美现代政府治理变迁的情境,原则明确、脉络清晰地呈现出公共管理理论和知识的连贯发展过程,简明而又深刻地阐释了若干重大历史事件对公共管理变革方向的决定性影响,全景式地勾勒了英美公共行政传统的形成和德国、法国、瑞典等欧洲国家公共行政的特点及其对现代政府治理的贡献与启发。在作者卓越的通俗化叙事的努力下,读者遇见了一系列促进政府治理质量改善、对当今全球政府治理具有奠基性意义的重大改革议题,例如:如何最好地确保公众问责;一个执行不力的政府,不管其构建了怎样的新理论,实际上都一定是一个不好的政府;地方政府更能察觉公众的要求,因此更有可能对他们的关切做出反应,行政体制改革方案可以将行政权力下放地方政府;公共管理者和公众都将继续努力应对因观点不同而产生的治理困境;等等。

公共管理学的性质,决定其不仅要探索政府治理的理论,也必须提供解决问题的方案,因此政府改革始终是公共管理学直面的科学问题和难题。本书围绕全球范围的行政治理改革和新公共管理实践，以回溯的视角和诊断式叙说，阐释和描述了政府治理不断完善和进步的几个关键特征。其一，政府治理改革具有渐进性，改革不能在任何意义上疏离政府的使命和价值，因为支配政府治理行动的那些深刻的原则是永恒的，行政改革是"不得不采用新的官僚方法和程序来履行新的职能和任务"。其二，政府改革是全球性的运动，任何现代化的国家都需要并期待一支政治上公正无私、恪守正直、得体、客观和任人唯贤的永久的公务员队伍，也都需要更有效的方法提升公共政策的执行能力。然而，无论是美国、不列颠还是欧洲其他国家，政府改革都必须结合地方性知识，结合自身的历史和文化传统。其三，政府改革是一个政治和行政双重因素交织的变革过程，将泰勒制等科学主义融入政府改革是行政效率的谋划；而政府改革又受到"治理"的深刻影响，突出的一点就是要在政府与市场的钟摆式晃动中确立目标和方案，新公共管理改革就是钟摆偏向市场一极时形成的政府管理方案。本书中基于这些关键特征而做出的精辟分析和论述，增强了公共管理学知识的通用色彩，可以原则性地对现代化国家政府治理行动给予指导。

如果说，关于政府治理行动的原则、制度和改革方案的理论和知识，尚不足以作为通俗读物的亮点，亦即非专业读者可能从中找不到与自己的链接，那么本书中有关福利国家、网络治理或新公共服务的内容，将会是邀请读者进入公共管理世界的名片，因为这些内容突出强调了在当今政府治理中，公务员以"多做多对"的伦理精神帮助公民实现他们的合法权益。与福利主义紧密相关的社会政策的制定，直接关涉政府如何解决就业难题，以及如何使得公众获得"免于贫困、疾病、无知、肮脏和懒惰的权利",公众免于痛苦的期盼及其达成度,相当程度上与政府治理质量密切关联。此外,网络治理使得政府治理体系更能吸纳社会力量的参与,进一步实现政策可找、政策可见的透明政府的发展。为此,"一批批高技能的公共部门专业人员正在接受培训,以取代旧的'官僚'形象",在公共管理者与公众之间形成更加友好的治理界面,由此成为公共管理变革的时代性追求和目标。应该说,这也正是公共管理学日益走向公共知识的一个反映。

本书尽管是一本通俗读物,但并不影响其成为公共管理的经典读本,经典之处就在于,隐藏在本书叙述视角、重大事件和实用案例之中的原则和理论,恰恰是决定公共管理学作为一门独立学科的关键知识,非专业读者借此可以与专业研究者为寻求共识而展开对话。在今天,一个学科的生命力不仅体现在其新知识的探究上,而且取决于这一学科是否拥有良好的公众形象。

总而言之,这本经典通俗读物主要呈现的是欧美现代化进程中政府治理知识的变迁,但从文明互鉴的立场来看,本书非常值得中国的公共管理专业研究者、公共管理者和其他兴趣爱好者阅读,从而在比较分析中为中国公共问题的解决提供更加有益的方案。如果说我们个人的发展和家庭的幸福越来越深刻地嵌入到政府的治理行动之中,那么关心公共管理学也就是关心我们自己的生活质量。

目 录

前　言　1

第一章　当代概述　1

第二章　从威斯特伐利亚到费城的旅程　15

第三章　全球范围的渐进式改革　24

第四章　现代福利国家的兴起　40

第五章　"新公共管理"走向全球　55

第六章　新行政时代　73

第七章　全球化与网络治理的兴起　83

第八章　公共管理的未来　90

索　引　95

英文原文　101

前　言

在当今的全球化时代,成为一名高效的公共管理者意味着什么?在本书后面的章节里,我们将邀请您加入我们,来一次公共管理专业和职业实践的旋风之旅。我们将沿着这条路探索这个专业和实践如何随着时间的推移从其开端发展到当今这个时代。在我们的历史调查过程中,我们将揭示一些基本的领导和管理原则,这些原则基本上界定了怎样才能成为一名高效的公共管理者。

什么是公共管理?为什么它如此重要?为了实现社会的集体目标,公民领袖必须学习如何组织和管理公共机构。更确切地说,公共管理可以说是一门管理和领导的"艺术",涉及发展和提供基本的公共服务,以维持现代文明。公共部门提供的服务涵盖了从公共安全和社会福利到交通和教育等领域,这是我们日常生活不可分割的一部分。比如,想象一下,如果没有公共服务和公用设施,如公共道路和高速公路、紧急医疗服务、信息网络基础设施以及水电,生活会是什么样子。很多时候,我们总是把这些基本的"公共产品"看作理所当然。我们大多数人只是简单地过着每一天,很少考虑或了解提供这些服务的复杂过程。更糟糕的是,我们常常将困扰现代社会的所有问题归咎于"大政府",把公共管理当局视为"懒惰的肥猫",这已经成为一种"时尚",司空见惯。

这种无情的特性描述在美国政治右翼最近发起的政治运动中得到了强化。然而,事实上,正是那些属于意识形态光谱的政治右翼和左翼的人在施加越来越大的政治压力,以图残酷地削减这些基本服务。全球各地的现代政府出于对更大程度紧缩经济的需要,也都被迫"用更少的资源做更多的事情"。这一趋势预计将持续到可预见的未来,因此将被视为在当今世界运作的公共管理者的"新常态"。公共管理者被迫在日益激烈的政治环境中工作,在这种环境中,政府被看作"问题的制造者而不是问题的解决者",公共管理者被迫彻底重新思考他们在当今的时代该如何进行治理。

随着大批婴儿潮时期出生的人退休,公共部门面临前所未有的挑战,这也为新一代合格的、训练有素的领导者和管理者打开了大门,让他们承担起这些不可或缺的政府职位。有抱负的公共管理者和领导者如果要成为这些就业机会的合格候选人,就必须了解公共部门的作用,以及在全球化时代如何重塑公共部门。最近,全球各地申请公共管理研究生和本科生课程的人数激增,就证明了这一点。

虽然我们知道有很多教科书和其他文献资源可以提供坚实和全面的与该专业相关的理论,但很少有人综合这些资料,使其变成简明扼要和易读的读物。我们邀请读者踏上一次引人入胜的旅程，探察一些重要的历史运动和趋势，为这个迷人主题的起源和持续发展提供信息。事实上，我们将带领读者探索这些趋势在世界不同国家和地区的具体表现。除了简单的概述之外，我们还将探讨当代一些最热门的问题，包括："政府是否应该像企业一样运营"，或者公共服务私有化是不是一个提高服务质量和降低纳税人成本的适当方法，以及政府为保护其公民免受恐怖主义袭击所做的监控努力是否会侵犯个人隐私和个人自由。

我们将利用我们的经验和知识专长精心编排我们的讨论，让我们讨论的方式与美国、加拿大、英国、欧洲和澳大利亚的读者产生良好的共鸣。此外，用来说明本书讨论主题的许多案例研究是专门为亚洲和拉丁美洲的读者量身定制的。为了让当代的公共管理者准备好迎接等待他们的巨大挑战，我们的论述侧重于公共管理专业的基本历史和背景。为了从本质上讨论这个高度复杂的话题，本书将为公共管理者提供实用的见解，帮助他们在面对当代困境时提出更好的问题。

为了与"牛津通识读本"通俗易懂的基调保持一致，我们在这里的讨论是选择性的和一般性的。我们将此书定位于吸引感兴趣的非专业读者，目的是向我们的读者提供引人入胜的概述，来说明这个非常丰富和高度复杂的主题。对本书简短讨论的主题有了基本了解之后，读者可能会准备更深入地研究这个主题。这些读者可以查阅本书末尾的参考书目和其他资料清单，这些资料将为他们提供更加细致入微的讨论和分析。

我们要感谢加利福尼亚州立大学北岭分校、南犹他大学、克莱蒙特研究生大学和加利福尼亚大学圣巴巴拉分校的同事和朋友为我们提供的宝贵支持。我们要特别感谢安德莉亚·基根和她在牛津大学出版社的出色团队。我们还想把最深的爱和感激给我们各自的家人：琼、妮可、伊安娜、玛蒂和亚历克斯。我们在撰写本书的过程中咨询了无数的人，我们感激不尽；书中存在的不足之处由我们独自承担责任。

第一章

当代概述

最近,在我们参加的一次大学招生宣讲会上,一名学生走近我们的一位教师代表,直言不讳地问道:"什么是公共管理?拥有该专业的学位我能找到什么样的工作?"这个看重就业的年轻女孩继续问道:"我的意思是说,我听说过这个专业,当然,每个人都听说过。但它到底是什么?教些什么?"这个年轻女孩提出了一个严肃的问题,她或许甚至没有意识到她无意中发现了一场正在进行的辩论,一场长期以来一直在学术界和从业者中进行的激烈辩论。这位教师迫于要立即做出回答就解释说:"公共管理涉及官员在向我们国家的公民提供基本公共服务时所进行的无数活动。"这位教师继续解释道:"公共管理者服务的范围从执法到城市规划,他们的工作地点可以在当地的市政厅,也可以一直到白宫的机构。简而言之,作为教师,我们的目标是为公共管理专业的学生提供公共管理服务所需要的专业指导和管理技能。"虽然这个简短的解释似乎让提问者对该专业有了一定了解,但肯定还有更多的内容要说。因此,我们邀请您加入我们,让我们一起更深入地探讨这个复杂而迷人的话题。

虽然"职业民事管理人"的概念通常被认为在历史上起源于四千年前的美索不达米亚帝国,但部落领导的原始形式可以追溯到公元前10000年的石器时代。事实上,正如文化人类学家赫伯特·S.刘易斯所指出的,"领导力是社会组织群体活动的一个基本要素……它处于或接近大多数政治生活、政治竞争和斗争的核心"。人类总是指望民事领导者来监督维持共同生活的群体所需的各种活动。可以肯定的是,民事领导者的角色在不同的文化中有很大的不同,这取决于他们应该履行的职责和他们所拥有的权力。无论是部落酋长、有权威的君主还是民主选举的官员,任何社会都需要民事领导者做出决定和动员实现其目标所需的资源。然而,民事领导者需要依靠大量的下属"官员"来实现这些目标。实现这些目标所涉及的无数"官方"活动可以统称为公共管理的"艺术"。

就其核心而言,公共管理是指由参与公共部门"治理"的文职官员所执行的一系列领导和管理的职能与任务。根据劳伦斯·E.林恩、卡罗琳·J.海因里希和卡罗琳·J.希尔的观点,治理涉及"制度、法律、规则、司法决定,以及约束、规定和提供公共支持的目标和服务的行政实践"。公共管理涉及我们日常生活的方方面面,包括了"街道层级"的普通官员日常所做的连续过程、例行公事、行动、行为和自行决定。因此,公共管理涉及的并不仅仅是更高级公职人员所负责的权威行动。事实上,有数以百万计的公共管理者在各个领域工作,如城市规划、公共交通、预算编制、政策评估、选举监测和监督、执法和消防,以及从医疗保健到失业援助和职业再培训的社会服务。正如那位教员向参加大学招生会的未来学生指出的那样,公共管理者的职位可以是一个国家的总统或总理及其内阁成员,也可以是一个地方市政的停车执法人员。

参与治理过程的公共当局和机构之间的互动高度复杂。例如,美国相对分散的行政系统包括一个国家级政府与五十个州级政府和近九万个在县、市、区一级运作的单位分享管理责任和权力。美国庞大的公共部门拥有数百万名公共管理人员,为公民提供从公共工程、儿童保护到食品安全和康复的基本服务。相比之下,英国拥有一个相对集中的系统,在这个系统中,国家级政府将特定的职能和授权委托给各种"国家级以下"的行政部门。英国的地方行政机构分布在三百多个区,这些区又分为都会区和非都会区。这些区由市长和区议会监督。从公共交通和住房到公共卫生和教育的各个领域,这些机构提供重要的服务。就其本质而言,治理与政治是交织在一起的。让我们更详细地看看这一点。

巨大的政治悖论

随着时间的推移,为应对公民的需求,公共管理人员的职能和授权成倍增长。寄希望于政府提供和管理越来越多的公共资助的学生贷款和支持小型私营企业的政府资源就是典型的例子。最大的矛盾是,在公民对公共部门服务的需求和期望不断增长的同时,公众对"政府"的满意度似乎在下降。一位著名学者甚至提出,美国公民希望严格限制政府通过更高的税收和与安全相关的监控干预他们的私人生活,同时又坚持要求政府在必要时增加支持以帮助他们。事实上,美国的民意调查全都认为,大多数公民对政府持有负面看法,他们通常将公共官僚机构与"浪费"和"低效"联系在一起。而且,并不只是美国这样。在2013年6月11日的美国有线电视新闻网(CNN)的一篇社论中,皮尤研究中心全球经济研究所主任揭示,虽然近75%的澳大利亚居民对他们的个人经济状况感到满意,但对政府的管理感到满意的不足50%。对"政府"和"公共官僚"的不满,也是许多欧洲国家越来越普遍的情绪。

"问责制"、"效率"和"绩效"等时髦词汇,已经成为风靡全球的"善治"运动的政治口号,也成为最近中间偏右的政治运动的主题,目的是推动财政紧缩并确保大幅削减政府资源。在某种程度上,这些情绪反映出公众对政府处理一系列引人注目的危机的方式越来越失望,而这些危机现在已经成为全球化时代现实的一部分。无政府组织实施的恐怖袭击或市场失灵(和大规模的系统性欺诈)导致的金融危机可能源自世界的某个地方,但它们可以迅速从一个国家蔓延到另一个国家,造成国家和地方层面通常都能深切感受到的毁灭性影响。这反映出公众的一种观点,即他们的政府"没有尽力保护他们"或事后未能有效应对,公众对政府的态度变得越来越消极。尽管危机的起源经常不在政府官员的管辖和控制范围内,公民却经常将这些灾难性事件归咎于"政府官员",他们发现这样做在政治上是方便的,并且对自己是个安慰,他们认为这些官员"在开车时睡着了"。令人尴尬的是,这些危机发生后的大量善后工作往往落在财政一直捉襟见肘的公共当局肩上。

当政治和行政发生冲突时

当代公共管理专业和实践的显著特征涉及一个永远令人

烦恼的问题，即做出决策的政治应该在哪里结束，与政治无关的管理和行政事务应该在哪里接手。当政治世界与行政管理程序发生冲突时，可能会出现一些有趣的场面。最近的一场高风险的政治对峙是这种现象的最显著例证之一。2013年10月1日，全世界困惑地看着美国政府近二十年来首次关闭。由于美国最高政治领导层之间无法达成一项关键的预算协议而陷入政治僵局，这场戏剧性的考验有可能使美国整个联邦民政管理陷入困境。由于国家公园、大多数联邦办公室被迫关门和国家航天计划被迫取消，近一百万公共部门的工作岗位岌岌可危。正如公开的估计所显示的，负面影响扩展到了私营部门，政府关闭每天造成近三亿美元的生产产出损失，威胁到美国脆弱的经济无法从最近的全球金融危机中复苏。

预算僵局并不是行政程序本身造成的，而是美国两大政党正在进行的激烈政治斗争造成的。两大政党关于提高债务上限以弥补2014年预算中330亿美元巨额缺口的决定意见不一。由于缺乏果断的行动，越来越多的人猜测美国政府将会拖欠主权债务。许多人担心长时间的摊牌会引发投资者恐慌，进而导致整个全球金融体系的崩溃。当最受尊敬的信用评估机构之一的标准普尔公司下调了美国的主权债务评级，潜在地限制了美国借入更多资金的能力时，投资者的担忧得到了证实。随着僵局一天天过去，人们对美国领导能力和行政能力的信心逐渐丧失。

事情怎么会变成这样？从政治上来说，两党很多人相互指责。立法机构中中间偏右的政党领导人将美国失控的债务问题归咎于他们所认为的巴拉克·奥巴马总统的巨大开销和他的左翼政治支持者。反对派领导人将预算僵局视为大幅削减社会支

> **方框1　美国医疗保健交易所**
>
> 2010年，美国立法者通过了政治上有争议的《平价医疗法案》。这项历史性的法案在2013年建立了"健康保险交易所"，这是一个消费者从一系列联邦认证的私人供应商那里购买健康保险的市场。该法案还允许各州选择建立自己的交易所，与其他州建立地区合作社，或与联邦政府合作。建立和管理医疗保健注册网站的过程给州政府带来了巨大的挑战。在启动的最初阶段，十四个州中有五个州建立了自己的健康交易所，预计将花费近2.5亿美元来解决注册网站中存在的问题。

出的谈判机会。与此同时，美国总统指责他的政治对手将预算过程作为人质，阴谋破坏美国历史性的《平价医疗法案》，即俗称的"奥巴马医改"（见方框1）。虽然最终达成了脆弱的预算妥协，避免了全面危机，但十六天的僵局表明了政党政治与政策和行政过程密不可分的程度。这进一步说明了破坏性的党派政治会如何扰乱整个国家的行政系统。

政府应该像企业一样运营吗？

在财政资源减少的情况下，"缩减"政府支出的政治要求不断增加，迫使公共机构承担新的授权、职能和任务。换句话说，各级公共机构正被迫"少花钱多办事"。对"更精简、更有效"的公共治理形式的无止境追求，迫使国家、地区和市政领域的政策制定者和公共部门管理者，越来越多地将重点从基于流程的实践向"经济合理化"的结果转变。例如，在过去的三十年中，公共管理者面临着调整其流程和服务提供方法的挑战，以便达到定量衡量的目标，如成本效益分析和其他基于绩效的标杆。事实上，公共管理紧张的一个主要来源是"公平"和"平等"的民主价值观与"绩效"和"效率"的市场价值观之间的持续冲突。

对公共部门的消极态度反映在越来越多的人认为"政府是问题制造者，而不是问题解决者"。在这种情绪影响下形成了一种流行的说法："政府应该像企业一样运营。"这场运动的先锋之一是英国前首相玛格丽特·撒切尔（1979—1990）。撒切尔认为，英国公共支出的增长在很大程度上归因于政府支出"不可控"的增长。因此，她厌恶增加税收来资助臃肿的政府机构的想法。英国现任首相戴维·卡梅伦也认为私营部门可以"做得更好"，他最近表示，国家安全领域之外的公共服务应该向一系列能提供更好服务的提供者开放。虽然政府和企业的联合行动对一个健全的社会至关重要，但是将商业的效率逻辑（为了最大化盈利能力）应用于公共部门是未能认识到二者各自的目的和功能从根本上说是不同的。简而言之，公共部门的存在是为了提供"公共产品"或须由整个社会支付费用的服务，任何人都不能被排除在外。这包括公共教育和公共道路等不可或缺的项目。相比之下，私营部门提供的商品和服务是在市场上私下出售并由个人消费的。

经济学家约翰·T. 哈维质疑将商业理念应用于公共部门是否合适，他认为，"并非所有盈利的东西都具有社会价值，也并非所有具有社会价值的东西都是盈利的"。例如，哈维指出，虽然许多私人出售和消费的物品，如真人秀或色情制品，在私人市场上可能利润很高，但它们没有社会价值，对一个运转良好的社会没有贡献。另一方面，军事防御、公共安全和普及教育等是不可缺少的，往往提供了巨大的社会价值，却没有给为此买单的公民带来直接的现金回报。

公共部门可以在适当的情况下采用某些基于私营部门的管理战略和做法，并取得巨大的成功。然而必须记住，政府机构和在其中服务的公共管理者与企业不同，他们必须对那些更广泛的利益群体负责，并受其他政府机构的监督。因此，将公共部门流程和服务的控制交给私营部门不一定妥当，例如将机动车记录或官方法庭文件部门的管理移交给私营部门进行文件处理和存储管理，就可能会潜在地损害公民的隐私权（见方框2）。此外，将这些基本职能外包给私人会使它们超出民主问责和监督的范围。

方框2 铁路私有化的失败

一些高调的私有化的失败推翻了"私营部门总是比公共部门更有效率"的流行观点。例如，国营的英国铁路公司在20世纪80年代被拆分并廉价出售给私人投资者。在新的安排下，私营的英国铁道公司负责监管轨道、信号和车站运营，而客运服务由28家独立的公司承担。私有化方案包括将一个整合的公共运输网络拆分成100多家独立的私营公司和分包商。结果，英国留下了一个高度分散的公共运输系统，无法对重要的交通安全设备进行必要的监督。这导致了一系列灾难性的事故，最终造成30人死亡，近400人受伤。

美国茶党在2009年跃上了全国舞台，出于对公共部门的蔑视及其通过累进税重新分配财富以资助社会服务的历史使命，发起了一场针对奥巴马"大政府"经济复苏计划和国家医疗保健计划的政治运动。这个团体包括共和党所谓的"右翼"成员，如南卡罗来纳州参议员吉姆·戴明特和得克萨斯州参议员特德·克鲁兹，以及明尼苏达州的米歇尔·巴赫曼和田纳西州的玛莎·布莱克本等国会代表。在茶党出现后不久，议程各异的反政府民粹主义运动开始在全球各地兴起，从"极右"到更极端的法西斯运动，例如英国的独立党（UKIP）、德国的新选择党（AfD）和希腊的"金色黎明"。

公共管理与全球动荡

如前所述，全球气候变化和全球恐怖主义给各级政府的公共管理者带来了巨大挑战。世界各国的地方公共管理者必须善于处理源自境外的危机。全球工业化和城市化的共同发展，给地方公共管理者带来了历史性挑战，迫使他们扩大责任范围和专业知识领域。事实上，世界上许多主要的大都市区都面临着城市密度激增和城市扩张带来的重大管理难题。由于现有的基础设施和市政资源很快就不堪重负，公共管理者面临着提出有效解决方案的挑战。与全球生产急剧扩张相关的碳基工业污染水平不断上升，引起了最近与气候变化相关的自然灾害的频率和强度增加。反过来，这些事件对大都市区造成了严重破坏，给地方管理者造成了巨大的困境。让我们简单看几个例子，说明与全球化相关的一些力量如何影响地方公共管理。

图1 水下的新奥尔良

在美国，市政官员是有权处置任何自然灾害或公共安全威胁的第一责任人。当国家和地方管理者在危机或紧急情况下缺乏必要的协调和沟通时，结果可能是灾难性的。在自然灾害卡特里娜飓风之后出现的管理崩溃就证明了这一点。2005年夏天，一场一级飓风在数英里外的海面上迅速转变为时速125英里的自然之力，肆虐了路易斯安那州南部海岸。无情的降雨和极端的大风袭击了新奥尔良市的周边地区，使80%的市区被水淹没（见图1）。虽然大多数城市居民在飓风登陆前已被成功疏散，但许多居住在偏远乡村地区的人却无法逃生，只能自我保护。随着水位持续上升，邻近的运河堤防开始漫溢，最终决堤，加剧了洪水的危险。随着一些地区的水位高达十五英尺，地方、州和联邦政府官员很快意识到，现有的救援计划和资源严重不足。当飓风最终平息，洪水开始退去时，官方对损失进行了调查。令人不寒而栗的估计揭示了令人清醒的现实：在最初的灾难中，有近三百人丧生，更多的人死于随后的洪水，或者等待救援的过程中。数百万人受伤、流离失所或无家可归。财产损失高达数十亿美元。

然而，正如世界很快就会看到的那样，真正的悲剧是由一场大规模的拙劣应急响应造成的，这将成为"政府无效"和"无能"的象征。事实上，一份2006年的政府报告后来证实，"联邦、州和地方官员未能预见到飓风登陆后的情况，延误了飓风登陆后的疏散和救援"。各级官员指导方针混乱，未能区分"正常灾害"和"大灾难"，未能识别和预告洪水的严重性。在防洪堤决堤后，混乱和沟通不畅导致关键疏散措施的实施推迟了近二十四小时。著名的公共管理专家唐纳德·凯特尔后来评论说："当面对卡特里娜飓风时，各级政府都失败了……笨拙的反应可能是美国历史上最大的行政失败。"

几乎所有的通信服务都在洪水中被破坏了，使得各级政府的行政人员和救援人员在将近四天的时间里无法在现场相互联系。更糟糕的是，当主要线路出现故障时，也没有应急方案。美国联邦紧急事务管理局（FEMA）局长迈克尔·布朗无法参与州长办公室和市长办公室之间的讨论。与此同时，国土安全局局长迈克尔·切尔托夫未能就如何处理灾害向布什政府提供"充分的建议和忠告"，从而延误了联邦援助。卡特里娜飓风提供了一个典型的例子，说明自然灾害加上行政愚蠢最终会导致一场历史性的灾难。公众的愤怒导致了对国家紧急救援流程的根本性反思。在随后的救灾工作中，各行政机构之间的协调水平得到了实质性的改善。

现在让我们来看看与全球工业化相关的一些世界上特大城市的过度拥挤,是如何给世界各地的地方政府管理者带来困惑和挑战的。例如,印度以城市为基础的大规模工业增长对该国来说是喜忧参半。一方面,这有助于该国总体国内生产总值的大幅增长;另一方面,这也给像孟买这样的城市的公职人员带来了管理上的噩梦,他们无法成功地管理该城市的一千三百万居民每天产生的大量污水和固体废物。描绘数百万城市贫民窟居民生活的生动画面,让我们看到了这个日益严重问题的棘手之处。

中国上海的城市规划者正在积极应对大规模民工潮带来的巨大城市密度挑战,这些农民工从农村地区源源不断地涌入城市寻找工业就业机会(见图2)。在北京这样的主要城市中心周围涌现的"卫星城"已经吸收了一些增长的人口,从而缓解了对市中心的压力。然而,这些地区不断涌入的新居民,使现有的公共设施和交通设施很快不堪重负。甚至中国更偏远的城市也经历了自己的人口爆炸。例如,随着人口的指数级增长,相对默默无闻的西南城市昆明的人口数量将在未来几年超过美国的一些大城市。将我们的注意力转向南半球,墨尔本的市政官员、商业领袖和城市规划者,正在努力解决不断增长的人口对新基础设施和社会服务的需求。预计到2025年,墨尔本的居住人口将膨胀至约五百万,到2050年将达到近六百五十万。在来自世界各地,尤其是亚洲的新移民浪潮的推动下,墨尔本的人口预计将在未来四十年以每周一千二百人的速度增长,这需要重大的规划举措来应对城市的教育、卫生、供水和交通设施的新需求。根据澳大利亚财产委员会的说法,这些新需求预计将包括:"到2025

年新增1万个托儿所、约3350张医院床位和5700间教室；到2050年要新增2.9万个托儿所、8600张医院床位和1万间教室。"

图2 城市密度挑战

正如我们已经看到的，公共管理是一个与现代生活密切相关的高度复杂和动态的课题。与此同时，在我们的故事中，我们仅仅触及了表面。回到本章开始时未来的学生所提出的问题，我们可以说公共管理是政治、政策和处理能力的交会点，涉及政府的政策和方案的设计与采用。最重要的是，它涉及执行这些计划所需的处理能力和领导力。简而言之，公共管理包括在现实世界中实施"公共政策"所需要的广泛的政治和处理过程。随着我们旅程的继续，我们将探索公共管理作为一种职业实践和一门相关学术领域之间的关系。正如我们将在本书的后续章节中看到的，这两者是不可分割地联系在一起的，是高度流动的和动态的。学术领域致力于教导公共管理者如何改善政府组织在执行其任务时的职能和运作。那些讲授公共管理的学者的目标是帮助公共管理者磨炼他们的批判性思维技能，使他们成为名副其实的"公众信任的监护人"。的确，民主有赖于此。

也就是说，在开始理解公共管理者在当今复杂世界中的作用之前，我们必须努力理解现代国家的演变，以及公共部门在其中不断变化的作用和职能。公民们现在可以用极快的网速获取几乎无限的信息来源，能够思考和质疑公务员以他们的名义所做的事情。虽然在谁应该负责确保这种信息的质量和准确性上可能有很多问题，但"透明度"的概念正让人们燃起对扩大已有的民主问责制的希望，并将其扩展到尚未扎根的领域。管理来自全球的信息是公共管理者面临的主要挑战。

全球各地的公共部门机构一直在通过寻找创新方法来提高其组织"能力"，以应对这些新的要求。因此，今天的公共管理者不得不采取灵活的策略和做法来应对不断变化的政治和经济情况。在许多公共机构中，一批批高技能的"公共部门专业人士"正在接受培训，以取代旧的"官僚"形象。因此，公共管理课程的学生入学率在美国、英国、欧洲大陆以及中国和澳大利亚都在迅速增加。

第二章

从威斯特伐利亚到费城的旅程

现在让我们回顾一下英美的行政传统,这些行政传统构成了当代的行政体系。正如我们将更深入探讨的那样,"公共"管理不同于其他形式的民政管理,它与民政管理是相互关联的。然而,在考察这些行政传统之前,让我们先简要讨论一下现代国家的基础和"人民主权"的出现。

人们普遍认为,当代治理和行政要归因于随着1648年的《威斯特伐利亚和约》而出现的现代国家的诞生。《威斯特伐利亚和约》宣告吞噬了欧洲中部大部分地区的毁灭性"三十年战争"(1618—1648)的结束,这个和约确立了新的国际公认的领土边界,并赋予新成立的主权国家治理其人民和土地的合法权利。国家可以根据其主权建立新的中央行政系统、标准和协议来管理国内和国际事务。

在英国、美国、法国和印度等国家,支撑现代民主行政体系的政治哲学植根于"人民主权"的概念。由于假定合法的统治取决于"人民的同意"(或被统治者的同意),因此人民主权和民主现在经常被认为是密不可分的。1642—1649年间的英国内战播下了人民主权的种子，这场内战导致了英格兰在位国王查理一世的下台。查理一世死后，英格兰被宣布为"联邦"，并在数年内置于下议院的最高统治之下。

英国哲学家托马斯·霍布斯由于在一定程度上受到1642年爆发的英国内战痛苦事件的影响，他厌恶内战和随之而来的无政府状态。霍布斯认为，社会内部的政治和社会稳定取决于强大主权当局的统一统治。因此他认为，一个政权的合法性来源于其维持政治统一和确保持久和平的能力。1651年，霍布斯完成了他最著名的著作《利维坦》，其中强调了通过社会契约来确保政治和社会秩序的重要性。在这种安排下，公民集体同意主权中央当局的统治。霍布斯是一个保皇派，他认为君主制最适合这些目的。尽管（让霍布斯高兴的）英国君主政体最终得以恢复，但它的主权将被削弱。

1688年的"光荣革命"使得向人民主权发展的缓慢旅程得以继续。从那时起，管理税收、皇室任命、战争、礼仪开支和政府预算的法律和行政权力，从君主的主权领域转移到了议会。在这一过程中，议会将承担政府的主要行政职能。由于不再受制于专制君主"武断"和"反复无常"的统治，这些革命性的制度变革使得政府的决策有了更大的合法性和可预测性。反过来，这些历史性事件最终会有助于在未来一个世纪塑造公共管理所具有的民主特征。事实上，尽管英国在形式上是一个君主立宪制国家，但代议制治理的规范和制度已经深深地植根于其政治体系之中。

启蒙思想家约翰·洛克断言，绝对君主制与公正治理的公民社会是不相容的,他为革命提供了一个煽动性理由,这将有助于确立人民主权的概念。洛克在1690年出版的《政府论二篇》中,为建立有限政府提出了一个充分的理由。洛克声称,如果所有合法政府的权威都来自人民的默认同意,那么所有的人就都拥有了自然权利,它独立于任何特定统治者或政权的法律。事实上,洛克坚持认为,"政府的目的"是保护"生命"、"自由"和"财产"。

洛克的哲学观点可以说是由他自己作为公共管理者的职业生涯所促成的。这位多产的哲学家担任了许多行政职务,包括在法国的外交职位,在法国议会担任贸易理事会秘书,在美国贸易和种植园担任专员。洛克认为,政治上不偏不倚的行政官员必须在法治范围内执政,以确保人民的利益和"公共利益"得到维护。然而,与此同时,洛克敏锐地意识到,公务员在履行他们的职能和授权时,应该在一定程度上拥有行政自由裁量权和自主权。

美国公共管理的早期传统

洛克关于有限政府和人民主权的思想影响了美国革命和美国宪法。美国人在脱离英国获得独立后,保留了英国法律、公共治理和行政的许多理念与传统。事实上,托马斯·杰斐逊在起草美国的《独立宣言》时从洛克的哲学观点中汲取了灵感。类似地,詹姆斯·麦迪逊在十年后制定《美国宪法》时也借鉴了洛克关于有限政府和社会契约的观点。反过来,正如我们将看到的,杰斐逊和麦迪逊各自对政府和行政权力的作用的观点,将最终塑造今天盛行的独特行政传统。

公共管理学者唐纳德·凯特尔对所谓的汉密尔顿主义、杰斐逊主义和麦迪逊主义传统进行了清晰的概述，并解释了它们与当代涉及公共管理和公民治理的讨论和辩论的相关性。开国元勋们认识到，一个强大到足以保护公民"不可剥夺"权利的政府，也有足够的力量剥夺这些权利，因此他们寻求在行政效率和个人自由之间取得正确的平衡。因此，他们一方面为促进有效政府的行政提案全力以赴，另一方面则试图对其权力施加严格的宪法限制。他们卷入了一场旷日持久的辩论，且一直持续到今天，争论的焦点是如何最好地确保公共责任。

由于汉密尔顿坚信需要集中的（联邦）国家权力，他被认为属于一个被称为"联邦主义者"的政治派别。杰斐逊对集中的国家权力持怀疑态度，并热情支持地方当局的主权权利，他被认为属于一个被称为"反联邦主义者"的敌对派别。在治理和行政上，介于杰斐逊和汉密尔顿观点之间的是麦迪逊主义的传统。让我们更深入地简要考察一下这些传统。

麦迪逊强调，需要在分立的机构中分离政治和行政权力，以防止政治权力的滥用，他采用了被称为"制衡"的制度。它包括将国家政治权力划分给三个同等的治理部门：行政部门（总统）、立法部门（立法机构）和司法部门（法院）。立法部门的主要责任是制定法律，行政部门执行法律，法院裁决法律。然而，实际上分配给三个部门的权力是部分重叠的，因此任何一个部门都不能对另一个部门施加过度的权力。例如，任何试图篡夺太多权力的总统都可能被立法部门弹劾，并被免职。同样，如果立法机关颁布的法律被认为是违反宪法的，美国最高法院可以推翻它们。在大多数情况下，立法部门和行政部门二者必须达成政治共识才能颁布法律。

为了保持总统和美国国会之间的权力平衡，麦迪逊的宪法设计在这些分支之间制造了一种永久的紧张感。麦迪逊的体系通常迫使决策者和管理者达成获得广泛支持的政治共识，以完成任何事情。平心而论，这一过程往往涉及旷日持久的谈判和长期斗争的妥协，造成政策和行政变革缓慢而令人沮丧。在极端情况下，这些紧张局势可能演变成激烈的破坏性冲突。我们在开篇就看到了一个突出的例子，那就是奥巴马总统和他在国会的党派对手之间2013年的预算僵局。读者会记得，行政部门和立法部门未能在这种情况下达成预算妥协危及了整个全球经济。然而，在分析美国的制衡制度时，重要的是要记住麦迪逊的重点，即要使暴政的威胁最小化，而不是最大化行政的便利。

相反，所谓的"汉密尔顿式"方法的追随者主张建立一个强大的"联邦"政府，这将激励国家团结，创造一个独特的美国政治身份。汉密尔顿认为，为了把事情做好，一个强有力的、相对独立的执行部门是行政系统良好运转必不可少的。汉密尔顿在《联邦党人文集》中提出，一个强有力的执行部门能够最好地确保国家安全和国内安宁，并促进法律实施的一致性。汉密尔顿在一篇文章中断言，"执行者软弱意味着政府执行不力"。无力的执行和糟糕的执行没有差别：一个执行不力的政府，不管它在理论上是什么，实际上都必定是个坏政府。

汉密尔顿和他的联邦主义者们提倡一种层级更为分明的自上而下的行政治理方式，支持扩大强有力的国家政府，因此被视为各州权利的潜在敌人。汉密尔顿认为，美国是一个潜在的工业强国，最终将挑战英国在全世界的霸权。为了实现他的设想，汉密尔顿指望中央政府资助国家的工业发展。为此,汉密尔顿后来利用他作为美国第一任财政部长的行政权力,建立了美国的第一家银行,以强化国家的独立战争债务,稳定其货币。汉密尔顿在试图集中控制国家财政的过程中进一步扩大了国家政府的权力。

杰斐逊直言不讳地批评大政府,不信任中央集权。事实上,他设想了一个共和国,将政治和行政权力基本保留给各个州。杰斐逊不太关注将国家建设成一个主要的工业强国,而是专注于为各州提供追求其独特命运的灵活性和自主权。汉密尔顿相信强有力的执行权的好处,但杰斐逊担心将过多的统治权和权威赋予一个行政办公室可能会带来暴政的潜在威胁。杰斐逊出于对强势君主式执行者天生的不信任,寻求将国家的最高权力委托给一个更具广泛代表性的机构。因此,杰斐逊迫切要求建立一个强大的立法机构,以便在国家政策制定和行政决策过程中能充分代表各州及其各自的利益。

杰斐逊的追随者宣扬有限政府的优点,他们认为政府是必要的恶,应以怀疑的眼光来看待,因此需要通过法治来调节。杰斐逊的传统与自下而上的民主联系在一起,国家以下各级政府享有广泛的自由,以符合当地规范和习俗的方式制定并实施政策。然而,杰斐逊派有时忽视了地方治理和行政中普遍存在的政治腐败倾向。事实上,杰斐逊时代就与分赃制度的诞生紧密联系在一起,在这种制度下,公共就业和政府服务的管理是建立在政治庇护而不是公平和公正的基础上的。事实上,当杰斐逊完成任期时,他的政府中有近三分之二的职位授予了他自己政党的成员。任命政党支持者担任联邦行政职务的做法通常被认为是合理的，认为这样做能形成"反应迅速的政府"。

具有讽刺意味的是，杰斐逊可能是最不信奉杰斐逊主义的总统之一。在1801年就任总统后，他立即表现出自己更像一个汉密尔顿式的执行官。在他任职期间，美国联邦政府的规模和权力急剧扩张。随着1803年从拿破仑的法国手中购买路易斯安那，杰斐逊的政府监督了近八十万平方英里领土的收购，2300万美元的收购款主要由伦敦的巴林银行资助，这是历史上最大和最有利可图的"土地掠夺"之一。这次大规模的收购最终将导致十三个新的州加入联邦。随着越来越多的人在西部定居，联邦行政机构，如联邦邮政局，需要大大扩展。自然，政府的规模和执行权力的范围也随着新的行政系统而增加。著名的历史学家亨利·亚当斯断言，杰斐逊运用的执行权力"比美国历史上任何时候都要完整"。由于许多汉密尔顿主义者赞同帝国需要皇帝来管理的观点，因此也默默地支持杰斐逊政府。

杰斐逊就职的目的是减少政府规模和国家的公共债务。杰斐逊从他的前任那里继承了近8300万美元的公共债务（大部分是独立战争遗留下来的），他立即被迫修改他的小政府议程。此外，他的政府后来被迫再借款1500万美元，以完成路易斯安那州的购买。杰斐逊深信，联邦政府需要少量的文职行政官员，这些官员是国家的服务不可或缺的，因此他从别处寻找必要的削减。杰斐逊强烈反对通过备战来维护国内和平与安全的主张，因此大幅削减该国的军费开支。随着军费大幅度削减，领土扩张带来的经济繁荣，以及提高富人消费的商品的关税，杰斐逊政府最终将国家债务减少了近60%。

反思当代公共管理

关于政府和行政权力的规模和范围应该多大才适当的当代辩论（无论是直接还是间接），反映了汉密尔顿和杰斐逊传统中概述的核心问题。与杰斐逊的推理一致的看法是，地方政府更能代表人民的性格，因此更有可能对他们的关切做出反应，政治运动应敦促将中央集权的主权政治权力和行政权力下放给地方各级政府。

在英国，越来越多的公民要求在该国某些地区实行更大的政治权力下放。为了回应公民对更直接代表和更大政治自治的要求，英国议会采取了一系列步骤，授予苏格兰国民议会、威尔士国民议会和北爱尔兰议会更大的行政和政治权力。2014年9月18日，举行了备受期待的全民投票，以决定是否让苏格兰成为一个独立的国家。虽然55%的选民投票赞成维持现状，但相当多的公民仍然强烈认为苏格兰应该获得独立。

许多当地的政治家和公民认为，密西西比州和南卡罗来纳州公民的特殊需求和文化价值观与纽约州和加利福尼亚州公民截然不同，他们一直在追切地要求更多的州权利。同样，正如我们在开篇看到的，美国类似于茶党的团体一直要求州政府完全控制从教育课程改革和生育权到枪支管制和非法药物使用等政策问题。

公务员和公民都将继续努力应对由不同的治理观点所形成的冲突而造成的行政困境。近年来，科罗拉多州、华盛顿州、俄勒冈州和阿拉斯加州已经将大麻的使用合法化，而美国联邦政府和其他许多州还没有这样做。自然，这在公共管理者和参与缉毒的多个机构中造成了广泛的混乱。例如，根据目前的司法划分，公民可以在大丹佛都市区拥有和使用大麻。然而，如果一个公民进入丹佛国际机场，因该机场由国家机场管理局管理，他/她就有可能会被指控犯有联邦罪。正如我们将在接下来的内容中所看到的，在全球化时代，国家和地方司法管辖区之间的行政紧张关系将变得越来越复杂。 26

第二章 从威斯特伐利亚到费城的旅程

第三章
全球范围的渐进式改革

"现代的"、"结构合理的"、层级森严的国家行政机构，与18世纪和19世纪政府权力的集中和欧洲帝国主义军事体系的扩张是一脉相承的。在18世纪早期，普鲁士帝国拥有高度复杂和定义明确的行政机构，这个机构延伸到军事和民事领域。在英国，现代文官制度的基础来源于东印度公司雇用的官员和代理人。东印度公司最初成立于1600年，是一家皇家特许的私人控股公司，后来发展成为拥有政治和经济权力的公司。在这一过程中，该公司建立了辅助性的民事行政办公室和复杂的军事指挥结构。事实上，这个体系后来被大英帝国用来统治次大陆的大部分地区。在19世纪出现的"民族国家"的政治权威和军事保护下，地区领土的巩固支持了科层结构行政系统的扩张。拿破仑统治下的法兰西的统一，1865年内战后"美利坚民族"的统一，1860—1870年朱塞佩·加里波第统治下的"意大利"的统一，以及1871年俾斯麦统治下的新德意志的崛起都是重要的发展。

虽然政治学家和历史学家对"现代民族国家"的特征和维

度仍在争论不休，但正如我们将在下文中看到的那样，它们不仅帮助奠定了现代公共管理专业和实践的基础，也为美国和西欧的现代社会福利制度奠定了基础。因此，公共管理者不得不采用新的"官僚"方法和程序来履行其新的职能和授权。正如我们将看到的，这些新的行政流程所植根的原则和方法是与所谓的"镀金时代"和"科学革命"相关联的。让我们首先讨论美国的进步时代，然后探讨最终塑造欧洲福利国家的渐进式改革。

美　国

正如我们在第二章中所讨论的，在杰斐逊时代开始出现了通过提供行政恩惠和公共服务以换取选票的普遍做法。随着这个国家的地域和人口持续增长进入下一个世纪，一个充满活力的公共部门蓬勃发展起来了。1824年的总统选举和安德鲁·杰克逊的上台，都与一场由美国南部的小农和北部的产业工人发起的新兴民粹主义运动有关。杰克逊自称代表"普通民众"，追求一种更具包容性的民主形式。这包括将选举权扩大到越来越多的人，代表着更广泛的社会和经济阶层。杰克逊宣称该国的政治议程和行政系统早已被该国的精英农民（即所谓的"种植园主"）、大商人和富有银行家所掌控，他接受了旨在吸引更加多样化的选民群体的民粹主义议程。

在后来被称为"杰克逊民主"的制度下，政党候选人是通过正式公开的会议提名的，而不是由党的精英们关起门来秘密选出的。随着越来越多的人可以越来越容易地参与美国的选举过程，传统上代表人数不足的社会阶层进入了政治纷争。政治候选人扩大了寻求政治支持和扩大公共服务范围的做法，以赢得不断增长的多样化选民的支持。"机器政治"嵌入了政治生活的各个层面。纽约市臭名昭著的坦慕尼协会和腐败的市长"大佬"威廉·M. 特威德，操纵着那个时代运转最为良好的政治机器之一。坦慕尼协会制造选票来换取政治庇护，许多人称赞它为代表人数不足的移民和贫困劳动者提供了必要的公共服务。然而，与此同时，这位邪恶的市长和他在市政厅的"政治亲信"因其肆无忌惮的做法而受到其他人的严厉批评。

到了19世纪中期，越来越多的美国人厌倦了分赃制度下产生的严重不平等，开始要求社会保护和全面的公务员制度改革。进步领袖们敦促联邦、州和地方政府共同努力，实施旨在改善社会正义和工作场所条件的新政策，特别是在该国的工业部门。这些新政策和法规包括确定保护儿童的法定工作年龄，限制工作日的小时数，以及颁布各种健康和安全措施。为了限制少数大公司对自由市场的垄断控制和操纵，进步派推动国会通过了1890年的《谢尔曼反托拉斯法》。

1881年詹姆斯·A. 加菲尔德总统遇刺，标志着被称为"进步时代"的新行政时期的兴起。进步人士试图用强调效率和公平的职业标准来取代与政治庇护相关的低效治理实践，在公务员就业领域进行相关的改革。例如，1883年《彭德尔顿法案》的通过促进了公务员委员会的成立，试图确保公共部门的雇用和晋升更加公平透明。《彭德尔顿法案》创造了新的程序和授权，最终帮助结束了许多腐败的习惯做法。到世纪之交，绝大多数公务部门的联邦职位都是通过严格的绩效体系任命和监督的。因此，对"训练有素"和"专业合格"的官员的需求不断增长，这极大地改变了公共管理的实践。

一些进步领导人寻求发展一个新的职业领域，探索创新的行政方法和技术，以改善官僚职能和运作。这场运动的主要先驱之一是伍德罗·威尔逊。威尔逊经常被称为"公共管理领域之父"，他认为治理的政治领域和行政领域应该是分开的、相互排斥的。威尔逊认为：政治是特殊利益的领域，而公共管理是为公共利益服务的；公共服务的职能应以符合最高专业标准和道德准则的方式来管理；公务员应该免受党派政治和政治庇护的腐败影响；政治应该限于与政策制定和采纳有关的事务，公共管理应该专门致力于"详细和系统地执行公共法律"。

　　威尔逊成了政治科学学术领域的重要人物。威尔逊的新"科学"致力于研究"那些深刻而永久的政治原则"，这些原则是在过去两千年中确立的，并已嵌入民主的文化和规范结构中。著名的公共管理学者，如弗兰克·古德诺也加入了讨论，他提出了关于政治决策应该在哪里结束，以及中立的管理和行政业务应该从哪里开始的重要问题。像威尔逊和古德诺这样的学者试图将组织管理思想和系统融入公共部门的实践中。这个新的跨学科领域最终吸收了许多资源，包括美国工程师弗雷德里克·温斯洛·泰勒领导的科学管理学派所强调的组织效率方法和德国社会学家马克斯·韦伯的理性官僚主义原则。

　　泰勒强调了标准化工作方法和简化生产流程以减少浪费和提高劳动生产率的重要性。在他的开创性著作《科学管理原则》中，泰勒强调使用系统分析和正规的工程学方法来研究工人的绩效和工作流程，从而改进其功能和运作。他相信运用经验观察和严格衡量的科学工具，管理者能够发现执行任何任务的最佳方法。泰勒认为，一旦发现了这些方法，就可以建立通用的最佳做法,然后应用到其他地方。

泰勒认为每个人都是独一无二的,因此拥有一套独特的技能。泰勒断言,对于管理层来说,识别每个员工的个人优势并指派"合适的人"去执行"合适的任务"是非常重要的。他进一步声称,那些向员工支付合理的工资,并允许他们定期休息的组织,将会让员工更加满意。反过来,这些做法将有助于提高生产率。诚然,许多组织选择性地应用泰勒主义的某些方面,而忽略了其他方面。泰勒的原则经常被错误地用来强迫员工更加努力地工作。结果,组织绩效的大部分责任被不适当地放在了员工身上。

随着泰勒的原则开始被整个政府机构所接受,越来越多的公务员被要求遵守严格的问责标准。此外,通过采用委员会和城市经理制度,泰勒的原则被引入市政管理。市政委员会由当选代表组成,他们担任市政部门的负责人。每个部门负责监督其管辖范围内的具体领域,如公共事业、卫生和警察。城市管理者系统由专业行政人员组成,他们被招聘来管理和监督市政管理中所涉及的众多职能和程序。城市管理者根据正式的商业惯例和组织原则运作,负责监督各市政部门所开展活动的执行情况。这些部门从市政府办公室到规划发展局等。20世纪20年代至50年代发展起来的"经典组织理论"的许多基本原则都是基于泰勒的工作。事实上,泰勒的"科学管理原则"一直影响着过去六十年的学术领域和公共管理实践。

英　国

自19世纪以来,如何发展和维护福利国家是形塑英国阶级政治的一个决定性问题。与美国不同,英国走过了一条漫长的、艰难的,有时甚至是有害的道路。在1601年的伊丽莎白时代引入的《济贫法》,旨在使英格兰和威尔士保护贫困人口的救济措施正式化。工业化带来了各种新的社会问题,需要系统地加以解决。随着时间的推移,与伊丽莎白时代原始法律相关的济贫规定已经成为英国富裕阶层的巨大财政负担。到了1830年,对穷人的社会援助已经上升到每年约七百万英镑。因此,在维多利亚时代采取了具体的改革,旨在降低这些成本。

在19世纪,大规模工业发展所造成的恶劣生活和工作条件,给人们的生活带来了沉重的负担。伦敦熙熙攘攘的工业部门产生的严重污染和有毒化合物,对工人及其家人的健康构成了严重危害。在这一时期,城市地区的过度拥挤和污染是疾病和健康状况不佳的主要原因。为了管理日益增长的与照顾病人和援助该国贫困人口相关的费用,议会通过了系统的改革。埃德温·查德威克等亲商的社会改革者坚持认为,良好的卫生习惯有助于"做好生意",从而推动了这一领域的重大变革。为了应对日益增长的公众压力,议会通过了1834年的(新)《济贫法》。这一举措大大降低了救济穷人的成本。另外,还采取了其他措施来管理采矿和制造业中危险行业的工作方法和流程。最值得注意的是,新的《济贫法》为越来越多的失业工人及其家庭建立了避难所,即所谓的济贫院。在许多情况下,住在这些设施中的家庭以衣服、食物和基础教育的形式获得基本的生活资料。虽然这些设施最初是为了提供临时救济,但许多租户在没有其他选择的情况下,最终不得不长期居住在此。对大多数居民来说,生活很艰难,无数身体健全的居民被要求做"苦役"以换取基本水平的援助。由于他们恶劣的生活条件,当时一些主要的进步活动家,如理查德·奥斯特勒,把这些济贫院视为"穷人的监狱"。

19世纪早期的《济贫法》进一步扩大了中产阶级和贫困劳动者之间的差距。这部分是因为,在缺乏任何系统的中央管理和监督的情况下,根据该法提供的许多服务在不同地方教区的管理是不平衡的,有时是非人道的。济贫法委员会是为了监督与1834年《济贫法》相关的服务管理和运作而建立的,由于公众对济贫院条件的不满和其他的临时滥用,导致济贫法委员会被废除。进一步的改革试图努力解决其中的一些问题。

1853年春,在时任财政大臣威廉·格莱斯顿的监督下,对英国民政管理系统进行了一次全面审查。在接下来的一年,一份被称为《杜维廉-诺思科特报告》的文件(以其作者查尔斯·杜维廉和斯塔福德·诺思科特的名字命名)建议对这一体系进行革命性的变革。这份报告除了建议举行考试以确保未来的公务员充分合格之外,还建议通过竞争性和透明的考绩制度来管理公务员晋升。根据彼得·亨内西教授的说法,拟议的改革将是"19世纪至20世纪最伟大的施政礼物:一支政治上公正无私的永久公务员队伍,其核心价值观是正直、得体、客观和任人唯贤,能够将其忠诚和专业知识从一届当选政府传递给下一届"。

从1906年到1914年,在首相赫伯特·阿斯奎斯和财政大臣戴维·劳埃德·乔治的领导下,实施了一系列历史性的社会福利改革。例如,在1906年,1901年《工厂法》中概述的安全条例被扩大到包括更多的工业。1908年,《老年退休金法》出台,将退休福利扩大到了七十岁以上、成年后大部分时间都在工作的人。事实上,该法为更广泛的渐进福利改革奠定了基础。一年后，第一个劳动力交换机构成立，以帮助失业工人找到新工作。同年，政府设立了发展基金，其目的是在衰退时期通过从农业到运输等领域的新基础设施项目创造新的就业机会。然而，这一时期最大的成就是阿斯奎斯政府颁布了国民健康和失业保险的法案。该法案规定了一系列福利，包括对身体和精神疾病的治疗。失业保险由工人和国家共同出资，扩大到就业极易受到经济结构变化影响的工人。劳埃德·乔治是这些历史性社会福利计划背后的政治策划者之一，他成功地使这些计划在议会获得通过。正如广泛记载的那样，劳埃德·乔治在起草英国1911年《国家保险法》时，是从他1908年对俾斯麦革命性的保险福利计划的研究中获得的灵感。

虽然之前讨论的许多改革在他们的时代是革命性的，但这些改革的覆盖面和保护对象是有限的，只为特定人群提供。例如，许多参加劳动力交换方案的工人只能从事非全日制临时工作。此外，工人必须用自己的收入支付国家保险费。然而，值得注意的是，在该法案通过后不到五年的时间里，估计有二百万工人享受了国家失业保险，另有数百万人享受了国家健康保险。也许更重要的是，尽管有缺点和局限性，这些渐进的发展在现代福利国家的演变中起到了至关重要的作用。

欧洲进步主义

19世纪80年代后半期，西欧的民族认同变得更加明显和突出。所谓的欧洲"民族国家"的出现，深刻地影响了公共管理的结构和范围。正如我们将看到的，强有力的中央政府和地方当局之间的关系比美国和英国更为和谐。让我们来研究一下区分这些管理系统的一些结构性差异。政治学者B.盖伊·彼得斯概述了三种西欧的行政国家传统,包括:法国或拿破仑时代的欧洲大陆传统;日耳曼或有机的欧洲大陆传统;斯堪的纳维亚的国家传统。

欧洲和美国一样,工业化带来的大规模城市化给社会和经济以及旨在帮助工作的和贫困的穷人的社会供给带来了巨大压力。尽管西欧和美国的改革运动都是与日益民主的国家同步发展的,但欧洲的进步人士却设想政府扮演一个更加家长式的角色。因此,欧洲人指望政府为他们的公民提供基本的经济保障,并将国家视为整个公民社会繁荣的保证。

与美国和英国的经历类似,事实证明,这一时期进行的进步改革在奠定现代福利国家的基础方面是具有变革性的。

法 国

1804年,拿破仑·波拿巴试图按照启发了法国大革命(1789—1799)的"启蒙"理想来改造法国的整个政治和行政系统。拿破仑试图把在这个国家封建历史过程中分散发展的各种地方性法规合并成一部现代的统一的民法典。在高度集权的国家官僚体制下,"国家"和"社会"之间的界限不像美国体制中那样明显。美国体制下的国家和州政府在宪法上是分开的,而法国的行政权力是统一的。法国的法律制度全面改革背后的首要原则是,确保每个法国公民都受到法律的平等保护。该法一经通过便在法国全境普遍适用,并最终扩展到居住在所有法国领土和管辖区的公民。的确,拿破仑传统最终影响了西欧各国以及北非和美国南部部分地区的法律与行政体系。

《拿破仑法典》的广泛范围涵盖了民事诉讼（1804）、商法（1807）、刑事诉讼（1808）和刑事制度（1810）等领域。特别是1808年行政法的重新设计，改变了整个法国的公务员制度。这部法典涵盖了从税收政策到银行和金融的方方面面，产生了新的行政办公室，并建立明确的管辖权和问责制。除了其他许多机构之外，还出现了审计法院、财政稽查总署和国务委员会。此外，拿破仑时代与世界上有史以来最雄心勃勃的行政公共工程计划联系在一起。法国精心建立的新的行政机构监督了新运河、港口和海港的建设与采购，此外还管理了综合道路系统的扩展，改善了法国与欧洲其他地区的联系。

进步理论家夏尔-让·博朗是拿破仑行政法典的主要设计师之一。博朗在1812年出版的《公共管理原则》一书中，概述了六十八条行政治理原则。这些原则中的大部分，涉及了行政组织为了更有效和负责任地运作而应该遵守的具体规则。这些原则适用于在各级行政部门任职的人，从部长到街道一级在法国无数的官僚机构服务的官员。博朗赞同威尔逊的观点，即"行政"应作为一套独特的实践和活动来研究，以区别于"政府"和"国家"所运用的政治方法。同样的，博朗的跨学科方法全面接受和使用了从自然科学中提取的正规方法，以及从社会科学和人文科学中收集的概念，以改善与行政治理相关的职能和活动。

1916年，法国采矿工程师亨利·法约尔引入了一种革命性的公共管理方法，这种方法被称为"行政管理理论"。法约尔在他的《一般工业管理》一书中概述了几个重要的原则，这些原则反映了管理大型组织所涉及的实际复杂性。"泰勒主义"强调使用基于经验科学的方法来提高员工在执行特定任务时的效率和精确度,而法约尔的方法强调管理在塑造和定义组织目标中的作用。法约尔断言,管理者必须承担起确保组织成功的责任,通过中央协调和控制来设定目标并培育不同部门之间的团结。法约尔认为,预测、规划和培训是提高组织效率和工作场所生产率的基本要素。法约尔的原则是灵活的,并普遍适用于任何组织环境。

德 国

1883年,德国第一任首相奥托·冯·俾斯麦提出了一个全面的进步议程。俾斯麦在普鲁士人和撒克逊人治下所发展的现有社会计划的基础上,推出了欧洲第一个社会保险计划。到1900年,德国工人有了医疗保险、退休金、最低工资、休假时间、失业保险、安全工作条件和免费的儿童教育保障。这些社会计划最初是为了满足德国工人阶级日益增长的需要和要求,但为社会福利制度的稳步扩大奠定了基础,并一直延续到第二次世界大战。

随着19世纪60年代德国的统一,政府的作用扩大了,需要一个更专业的政府行政部门来管理和实施新的社会计划和方案。正是在这种背景下,德国-奥地利公共管理学院首次出现。这场学术运动的领军人物之一是洛伦茨·冯·施泰因(1815—1890)。施泰因采用跨学科的方法研究公共管理,利用不同领域的人类知识,旨在改善行政治理的实践。施泰因通过他的题为《行政理论》的大量注释,试图将公共管理提升为一门"系统科学"。为了使这本"主要著作"中概述的原则广泛地为教师和学生所理解,他后来出版了他的《行政理论手册》。施泰因认为,应该通过考察国内和国际安全、外交、预算和财政等领域来研究和分析国家的行政活动。他建议,将这些不同的研究领域集中在一个单一学科之下,以服务于社区利益和保护公民个人权利的方式来改善国家行政机构的内部运作。

德国社会学家马克斯·韦伯的著作改变了组织理论和行政科学。如前所述,工业革命和国家扩展激发了全新组织模式的发展。由于需要协调大型公共部门和私营企业复杂的操作与功能,导致其组织结构发生了根本性变化。韦伯的官僚主义概念就是在这种背景下形成的。韦伯断言,现代组织需要采用基于正式规则的合理的官僚流程和程序,配备有适当技能、训练有素的人员的专业分类系统,以及结构良好的劳动分工。在韦伯模式下,职业官僚在行政职位上的任命和晋升是基于他们的技能和专业水平。为了执行高度专业化的任务和职能,官员们需要接受专业培训和教育。

韦伯在他关于官僚主义的开创性著作中,描绘了构成他的"理想"官僚原型的关键组织原则。对韦伯来说,官僚机构是将政策决定转化为具体行动的工具。因此,官僚机构的作用是通过客观、高效和标准化的决策过程来确保政府政策的有效实施。

韦伯并不认为官僚机构的实施是一种民主行为。事实上,他认为多元化的决策形式往往导致政策执行和实施方式的不一致。因此,韦伯认为,政策决定应该通过权威的决策过程,使用精确的执行方法来实施。在韦伯模式下,根据公法制定的政策和法规通过科层组织的办公室和部门进行管理。同样,正式的规则是通过严格的指挥链来执行的,例如以经理和工人向指定主管汇报的方式。

韦伯敏锐地观察到，由政治官员制定的大多数政策很少会非常明确地说明行政官员实施这些政策应采用的方法和手段。相反，他指出，大多数法规都是用宽泛且经常是模棱两可的语言写成的，这给了行政机构及其内部的公共官僚很大的自由，以解释何时以及如何执行这些法规。因此，韦伯断言，官僚机构的实际权力在于他们控制公共政策日常执行方法的能力。韦伯的原则已用来定义现代官僚组织的结构和角色。韦伯的"理想"官僚模式的特征是一套基本的组织原则，见方框3。

> **方框3 韦伯的官僚组织原则**
>
> 　　办公室层级：机构办公室按明确的层级安排；权力和权威建立在明确的指挥链基础上，每个办公室由更高一级的办公室监督，从而保证严格执行并确保官僚机构的权威。
>
> 　　固定的劳动分工：官僚组织中的任务被划分为不同的职能领域，每个领域都有必要的权力和批准权限；基本上每个办公室都有一个管辖区域，并由一套职责和权利来规定与治理。
>
> 　　合理合法的权威：正规的任务和程序确保了执行的一致性和对官僚行为的监管；他们的权威完全来自他们的职责，而不是来自某种私人地位，他们的权威只存在于履行这一职责所需要的范围。
>
> 　　非个人化：官僚管理是基于理性的非个人化的应用规则，并要求所有较低级别一致地执行最高级别做出的决

定；规则和控制被统一应用，以防止按官僚的个人偏好支配行为。

按资格任命：官僚职位的任命取决于专业技能和能力的测试，而不是地位或庇护的考虑；雇用和晋升基于优秀品质、技术资格、能力和表现。

职业精神：官僚是职业官员，拿固定的薪水；因此，他们并不拥有自己管理的单位。

独立无党派：官僚们的个人信仰和生活与他们的职业生活截然分开；行政是在持续的基础上进行的，而不是简单地根据个人和意识形态信仰的领导指令。

资料来源：肯·约翰逊，《根据马克斯·韦伯：历史原则》，载于《破除官僚主义》；斯特拉·Z. 特奥杜卢和克里斯托弗·柯菲尼斯，《游戏的艺术》，第170—171页。

斯堪的纳维亚

斯堪的纳维亚的公共管理传统是盎格鲁-撒克逊和日耳曼传统的混合体。19世纪早期，瑞典是欧洲工业最不发达的国家之一。这个国家独有的富有精英阶层和大量贫困农民之间的差距非常明显。然而，随着瑞典的工业化和国家财富的增加，富人与穷人之间的收入差距大大缩小。瑞典的工业化比许多欧洲国家要晚。因此，富裕的土地所有者、实业家和工人阶级之间的紧张关系与激烈的阶级冲突没有像英国那样的国家明显，一些学者令人信服地论证了这一点。在工业化相对较晚的欧洲国家，农民和工人阶级群体往往更强大，因此被其他强大的经济阶层视为更平等的伙伴。19世纪，在塑造瑞典民族国家的政治发展过程中，不同利益的相互包容促进了雇主和工人跨阶级联盟的形成。这些发展有助于形成制定国家社会政策的政治文化和机构。瑞典的大量社会服务都是在地方一级组织和管理的。这种安排有助于在瑞典公民和提供这些公共服务的公共管理者之间建立更密切的关系。此外，瑞典私营企业和公共部门之间的政治紧张关系在历史上并不像美国和英国那么明显。

到19世纪中期，瑞典正经历着许多与日益增长的工业化相关的痛苦的影响。瑞典政府于1842年推出的最早的社会服务之一是义务初等教育。随着瑞典民族国家在19世纪末期的稳固建立，雇主和工人共同支持扩大由国家政府提供的社会保险。

1889年，瑞典社会民主工党（SAP）成立，它的主要议程是强调普选和八小时工作制。尽管党内温和派和更极端的左派在如何最好地实现这些目标上存在分歧，但最终达成了普遍共识。此外，该党相对温和的进步目标吸引了该国的主流选民。

为了回应日益高涨的社会改革的民粹主义情绪，瑞典议会在1891年到1894年间通过了重要的社会保险立法。瑞典政府后来通过各种基于税收的现金福利计划提供广泛的公共服务和公共就业。1882年，瑞典国民政府采取了新的改革措施，以消除强加给小规模雇主的不公平的税收负担。1913年的法案将统一费率养老金福利扩大到所有六十七岁及以上的瑞典公民。1914年，国家失业委员会作为第一次世界大战特别管理项目的一部分而成立，成为在接下来的二十年里管理瑞典劳动力市场政策的主要行政机构。其主要目的是通过为各种公共工程项目提供财政和行政支持来减少失业。同年，瑞典国家政府开始为地方当局管理的穷人救济方案提供补充资金。

19世纪下半叶,工业革命和中央集权民族国家的出现,极大地改变了政府和社会之间的关系。在这一历史时期,公共服务和福利大幅增加。自进步时代以来,公民对政府的期望大大提高了。失业和社会保险、公共交通、公园和图书馆都是民主社会运动的产物。随着20世纪的到来,社会继续变得更加复杂,导致了额外的公共服务和监管的发展。因此,提供这些新的政府服务的行政过程和程序变得越来越专业化与官僚化。在这一过程中,政府在保护和促进公民的经济与社会安全方面承担了新的责任。

第四章

现代福利国家的兴起

让我们继续探索公共部门的演变和现代福利国家的兴起。我们讨论的历史背景始于20世纪20年代末和30年代初席卷全球的毁灭性大萧条。工业化国家的领导人无助地看着他们国家的资产价值似乎在一夜之间蒸发。与此同时,民族工业崩溃,数百万公民发现自己陷入失业和贫困。正如我们将看到的,这些可怕的事件将迫使西方民主国家的决策者开发新的行政系统和治理方法。

大萧条被认为起源于1929年10月的美国股市崩盘,并迅速成为20世纪最普遍的经济危机。消费者支出和投资骤降,导致工业产出大幅下降。随着经济状况的恶化,无数工人被解雇了。流动资产价值的大幅缩水导致资本市场枯竭。糊涂的政府匆忙制定了一系列保护主义政策,试图保护其国内市场免受进一步的国际传染。这些措施主要采取以邻为壑的政策形式,如进口关税和货币贬值。采用这些权宜之计似乎让情况变得更糟。到20世纪30年代中期,世界经济陷入了严重的经济萧条。由于没有任何总体的行政机构或连贯的政策策略，导致受影响的各国人民之间在管理国家救灾物资的方式上存在巨大差距。随着越来越多的公民陷入进一步的困境，西方政府面临着强大的政治压力，不得不采取激进的永久性解决方案。

尽管全球大萧条的确切原因仍有争议，但英国经济学家约翰·梅纳德·凯恩斯所信奉的经济思想受到了广泛关注。凯恩斯断言，经济以非常特定的方式循环运行。他认为，总产出以及随之而来的就业是总需求的函数。因此，他将失业率上升归因于经济中私人资本投资和支出的短缺。凯恩斯将这一现象归因于目光短浅的私掠者，他们的投资决策往往受到非理性预期和对未来盈利能力担忧的引导。他断言，负面预期会导致投资支出下降，从而导致需求和产出下降，进而导致失业率上升。

凯恩斯的思想极大地促进了被称为"宏观经济学"的专业的出现。这一新专业将关注点从个体转移到作为一个整体的国家中经济行为主体的总体行为。凯恩斯主义经济学家认为，各国政府有可能收集和分析大量经济数据，并在危机发生前预测危机。有了这些知识，政府就可以通过使用特定的财政政策工具来干预经济。例如，政府可以在经济衰退开始时增加公共支出，以帮助刺激增长，并在遇到经济繁荣时减少政府支出以减轻通货膨胀的压力。西方工业化国家的政府后来采取了一整套旨在防止未来危机的新监管体系和政策。

从美国到欧洲，再到日本和澳大利亚，工业化世界的各国政府广泛应用凯恩斯主义思想，导致许多人将1945年至20世纪70年代称为"管理资本主义的黄金时代"。富兰克林·D.

罗斯福和林登·B.约翰逊总统时期采纳的美国的"新政"和"伟大社会"计划、瑞典社会民主主义的方案,以及英国工党自1945年以来推出的福利方案,都反映了西方民主国家共有的历史性政治共识(表1)。这一时期的特点是发展汇率制度以促进稳定的国际市场,发展福利国家以保护劳工和贫困劳动者。让我们来看看在特定国家中影响现代福利国家兴起的一些条件。

表1 选定国家引入各种社会服务的年份

	养老金	失业保险	病假工资	医疗服务
德国	1889	1927	1889	1883
英国	1908	1911	1911	1911
瑞典	1913	1914	1914	1914—1946
美国	1935	1935		1965

美国前国务卿罗伯特·B.赖克在《超级资本主义:商业、民主和日常生活的转变》一书中,对"管理资本主义的黄金时代"进行了令人称道的概述:"经济是建立在大规模生产的基础上的。大规模生产是有利可图的,因为庞大的中产阶级有足够的钱购买可以大规模生产的东西。中产阶级有钱,因为大规模生产的利润被大公司及其供应商、零售商和雇员分享。后一个群体的讨价还价能力因政府的行动而得到加强和强化。几乎三分之一的劳动力属于工会。通过(对铁路、电话、公用事业和小企业的)监管和补贴(价格支持、高速公路、联邦贷款),经济利益也遍布全国,惠及农民、退伍军人、小城镇和小企业。"

德　国

德国是最早对20世纪30年代经济危机做出反应的国家之一，出台了一系列新的工程和项目的支出举措，旨在直接缓解该国严重的失业问题。然而，在战前几年，德国福利政策的面貌和该国对大萧条的反应发生了戏剧性的转变。例如，失业保险被取消，取而代之的是更广泛的公共工程项目。

战争结束时，德国被分成两个独立的国家。西德与西方列强结盟，而东德则与东欧苏联集团结盟。这些国家有着截然不同的政治和经济制度，以及截然不同的行政结构和福利国家模式。东德采用了受苏联启发的指挥和控制——自上而下的中央集权——的行政模式，而西德则采用了与大多数西方民主国家类似的更加以公众为中心的行政体系。

在战争结束后的几年里，西德领导人面临着必须将大量难民、退伍军人和受害者融入社会的挑战，被迫重新考虑和重建该国的整个社会福利体系。1949年，历史性的社会福利立法作为国家新宪法的主要部分被引入，这个新宪法被称为"基本法"。《基本法》通过建立一个"社会国家"，保证向每个公民提供一系列的社会保护。在许多方面，行政架构受到第三章讨论的"俾斯麦式福利国家"的启发。《基本法》授权在全国范围强制执行福利国家的关键要素。与此同时，法律允许地方政府自行决定某些社会服务的管理方式。

从1950年到1969年，西德经历了飞速的经济增长，这为其社会福利体系的大规模扩展提供了资金。一个高度复杂的公务员系统负责管理和监督大量的公共服务。虽然西德与美国等国家一样致力于民主和市场经济,但西德让政府在国家经济事务中扮演更重要的角色。虽然市场仍然是德国社会分配大多数资源的主要机制,但福利国家在缓和与无限制的自由市场竞争相关的许多负面后果方面发挥了至关重要的作用。根据政治左翼和右翼之间的"历史性妥协",德国领导人采纳了"社会市场经济"。在这种安排下,国家通过向工人提供各种公共资助的社会保障,在促进企业与劳工的工资妥协方面承担了正式角色。一些社会政策措施是通过集体谈判过程实现的。例如,这些措施包括向更多的公民提供社会保障,增加向工薪家庭提供的公共住房数量,以及采用雇员带薪休假的规定。新的立法还规定定期调整公共养老金,以反映工资和薪金的变化。

在20世纪50年代,法定健康保险扩展到更大的公民群体,包括学生、农民和残疾人。到1960年,公共和私人卫生总支出占德国国内生产总值的4.7%。然而,随着20世纪70年代医疗费用的飙升,政府感到有必要制定一项《医疗费用控制法》。被称为"一致行动"的联邦卫生财政和预算委员会得以成立,其目的是监督一系列成本控制措施。由于它缺乏足够的政治权力来实施任何严肃的成本控制措施,其活动被证明在很大程度上是象征性的。

瑞 典

在第二次世界大战结束后的头三十年里,瑞典因维持了资本主义世界最全面的福利体系之一,同时又拥有高水平的生产率和经济增长而受到称赞。在1932年至1976年间,一系列中间偏左的社会民主政府一贯支持扩大社会福利。该国的政治右翼和左翼人士形成了广泛的政治共识，走到一起支持共同的公共政策议程。最值得注意的是，劳工和商业团体在工人养老金、劳工工资和公司税等领域达成了历史性的妥协。结果，瑞典工人享受了一些在欧洲任何地方都没有的最慷慨的养老金，而该国的企业和股东则受益于工业化世界中最低的公司税率。

第二次世界大战后，随着瑞典工业的发展和经济的繁荣，社会民主党政府继续支持瑞典福利国家的扩展。因此，瑞典的公共部门官僚机构和行政系统在规模和范围上都有所扩大。不可避免，公共开支承受了额外的压力。事实上，公共部门支出占国内生产总值的比重在接下来的十年里持续稳步增长。例如，1955年的《国家保险法》将医疗现金福利（由疾病基金、税收和政府补贴资助）扩展到所有瑞典公民。在瑞典政府支持的集体谈判制度下，公共教育、慷慨的养老金福利、全面的医疗保健和失业者社会保险都得到了扩展。这些成本高昂的社会福利主要通过工人边际收入的累进税和雇主的直接缴款来提供资金。

随着瑞典社会福利体系在整个20世纪60年代和70年代的持续扩张，行政成本持续攀升。结果，沉重的财政负担加在了该国纳税人身上，瑞典公民成为资本主义世界中纳税最高的。随着时间的推移，瑞典选民不出所料地对政府的财政管理策略和高税收不再抱有幻想。社会民主党在执政近四十四年后的1976年的大选中最终接受了失败。倾向于保守主义的新政府，决心降低社会民主党近半个世纪建立的瑞典福利国家的高昂成本。然而，保守派领导人发现在政治上无法兑现他们的承诺。社会民主党在1979年的选举中重新掌权，并发誓要恢复他们对瑞典人民的承诺。仅仅在保守派掌权三年后，社会民主党重新掌权，享受了十多年不间断的统治。在整个20世纪80年代，瑞典人继续享有高生活水平和慷慨的福利与服务。超过30%的劳动力受雇于公共部门。也许同样令人叹服的是，国家近60%的国内生产总值花在了福利供给上。尽管在20世纪80年代中期，面对公共部门赤字和通货膨胀的增加，左倾的政府控制政府支出的政治压力越来越大，但社会民主党几乎没有做出调整。事实上，他们设法增加了儿童福利津贴，延长了失业救济。尽管他们最终被迫接受了在计算某些社会福利的基础金额时采用适度的成本控制措施，但瑞典的福利国家在1982年至1991年间基本保持不变。

美 国

　　1929年股市崩盘后的那几天，被证明是美国历史上最黑暗的日子。国家金融市场暴跌，数百万人失业。1932年富兰克林·D. 罗斯福的当选和"新政"的推行，以历史性的规模重塑了美国的社会福利政策。在罗斯福上任的头一百天，这位财政头脑清醒的总统推出了一系列旨在减轻危机影响的温和政策。然而，在接下来的八年里，他的政府采取了一系列更加雄心勃勃和积极的政府主导的举措，旨在稳定该国的经济。为了创造新的就业机会，提供新的水力发电资源来刺激经济，罗斯福与国会合作，批准为田纳西河流域管理局（TVA）提供资金。这个联邦所有的公司成立于1933年，成为国家的第一个区域规划机构。田纳西河流域管理局雇用了无数的工程师、土木规划师和工人，监督施工和管理大规模基础设施项目，包括旨在促进农业地区新发展的水坝和水道。与此同时，实行农业补贴以帮助提振在1929年崩盘期间下跌的大宗商品价格。

随着1935年《国家工业复兴法案》的通过,工人们被赋予了一系列新的集体谈判权利,这使他们能够组织起来争取更高的工资、新的福利和更好的工作条件。然而,最重要的是,该法案建立了一个新的由联邦政府支持的公共工程管理局。这在规模和范围上都是前所未有的,成为罗斯福的全面政府主导的"需求管理"计划的重要组成部分,以振兴经济。近六十亿美元被用于资助大型公共工程项目,包括建设新的公路、水路、桥梁、医院和教育设施。大部分资金是通过与私营企业的合同发放的,以支持私营企业的增长,创造新的就业机会,并提高消费者购买力。

在同一时期,罗斯福建立了公共事业振兴署(WPA),作为他的国家经济复苏宏伟蓝图的一部分。公共事业振兴署也许是最著名的"新政"项目,它最终为那些原本会被边缘化的人提供了各种就业机会。公共事业振兴署的大部分劳动力由非熟练工人组成,他们受雇从事小型建筑和改善项目。在社会工作者哈里·霍普金斯的领导和监督下,创造了数百万就业机会,包括与公共道路、政府建筑、公园和娱乐以及重新造林有关的无数项目。然而,许多美国人被降格去从事卑微和不重要的工作与任务。此外,政府委托制作了数千幅壁画和雕塑,装饰全国各地的公共建筑。额外的资金被指定用于戏剧和表演艺术。公共事业振兴署后来作为1939年《重组法案》的一部分被置于联邦工程署之下,直到1943年被完全撤销。

美国福利体系的建立成为新政的最高成就。1935年,罗斯福签署了《社会保障法案》,为数百万退休的美国人提供公共养老金支持,并建立了美国第一个国家失业保险计划。《社会保障法》不仅是为了防止痛苦,也是为了减轻痛苦。该方案的设计者试图通过向那些急需救济的人提供政府转移支付来改善已陷入贫困的人们的生活。与针对穷人的救济方案相关的大部分资金是通过1935年的《受抚养子女援助法》提供的，该法建立了后来被称为"受抚养子女家庭援助"（AFDC）的计划。

"新政"的政策和项目推动了美国联邦政府的扩展。很快变得明显的是，行政部门需要重组，以便成功地执行其许多政策和授权。一个行政管理特别委员会得以成立，俗称布朗洛委员会，以创建一个结构更加严密、管理更加一致的行政机构。罗斯福总统邀请著名的公共管理学者（前纽约市官员）卢瑟·古利克帮助组织这项全面的工作。罗斯福在制定改善美国公共管理系统的功能和运作的策略时，曾征求过古利克的意见。

1937年，古利克和他著名的英国同事林德尔·厄威克发表了与古利克在布朗洛委员会的工作有关的"行政学系列论文"。古利克和厄威克在弗雷德里克·泰勒强调的"最佳途径"的科学原则和方法，以及亨利·法约尔对行政管理的功能分析的基础上，提出了管理的七个基本功能。这些基本职能缩写为POSDCORB，包括规划、组织、人员配备、指导、协调、报告和预算。古利克和厄威克所讨论的管理的七个基本功能的特征如下："规划，即概括地制定出需要完成的事情以及完成这些事情的方法，以实现为企业设定的目标；组织，即建立正式的权力结构，通过这种结构来安排、定义和协调工作，以完成确定的目标；人员配备，即引进和培训员工并保持良好工作条件的人事职能；指导，即做出决定并将其体现在具体和一般的命令与指示中，作为企业领导者的持续任务；协调，这是最重要的职责，将各个部分的工作相互关联；报告，即通过记录、研究和检查，让负责人了解正在发生的事情，包括让主管和下属都了解正在发生的事情；预算，所有的事情都要有预算，做出计划、核算和控制。"

美国加入第二次世界大战创造了数百万个就业机会。战后几年，美国工业基础完好无损，在工业生产率方面领先世界。随着美国经济在整个20世纪50年代蓬勃发展，失业不再是一个政治问题。然而，到了20世纪60年代，公众对美国财富分配不均（尤其是在南部农村地区和北部城市）的担忧日益加剧，激发了国家的进步政治家们回到扶贫问题上来。在约翰·F. 肯尼迪和林登·B. 约翰逊的民主党总统执政期间，通过了一些具有里程碑意义的公共部门方案，旨在帮助美国工作的和贫困的穷人。约翰逊政府的"伟大社会"和"向贫困开战"计划成为这一努力的核心。推出了一项主要的福利计划——医疗保险制度，保证六十五岁及以上的人享有医疗保险。不久后又公布了医疗补助制度，将基本医疗保险扩展到贫困的美国家庭。在接下来的几年里，引入了更多的联邦方案，从住房补贴和学校午餐方案到家庭计划和妇女支持服务。联邦政府试图通过向儿童及其父母提供额外的公共服务来打破贫困的恶性循环。例如，1964年的《平等机会法》为教育和职业培训计划提供了联邦财政支持，并为早期教育计划，如"启蒙计划"创造了新的资金来源。

> **方框4　知识巨人的冲突**
>
> 　　1952年，《美国政治科学评论》刊登了一篇文章，引发了当时公共管理领域两位重量级人物德怀特·瓦尔多和赫伯特·西蒙之间的激烈讨论。备受关注的瓦尔多-西蒙之争有

助于明确该领域中日益增长的争论：一种是基于事实、"硬科学"导向的方法，强调"情况是什么？"；另一种是规范的调查路线，强调"要做什么？"在《美国政治科学评论》发表的题为《民主行政理论的发展》的文章中，瓦尔多强调了"科学的局限性"，尖锐地挑战"效率是我们科学的中心概念"的主流信念。瓦尔多坚持认为，"效率"不应该被视为一个普遍的公理，而是一个有争议的价值问题，必须在哲学的基础上进行探索和辩论。事实上，瓦尔多认为，"现有的科学技术不适用于研究"他所认为的公共管理的基本要素，即"思考"和"重视人"的问题。瓦尔多推论道："价值问题不适合科学处理。"相比之下，西蒙试图强调一种基于经验和科学的方法来进行行政分析和决策。这样做时，他断言，逻辑实证主义驱动的行政"科学"应该优先于基于价值的方法。西蒙通过他关于行政行为的著作，将自己视为一个组织理论家，而不是一个纯粹的公共管理学者。事实上，他后来被誉为现代（基于科学的）组织理论的领军人物之一，无论在公共管理领域之内，还是在此领域之外。

在20世纪60年代末和70年代初，与许多这些社会计划相关的费用开始超过现有的财政手段。政府出现了巨额赤字，并增加了税收。理查德·尼克松总统的保守派领导层抨击约翰逊的"向贫困开战"是政府开支失控的一个根源。此外，米尔顿·弗里德曼和赫伯特·斯坦等保守派经济学家让尼克松政府相信，约翰逊时代实施的许多社会计划助长了福利依赖的文化。

20世纪70年代被证明是美国历史上的一个动荡时期。在此期间，美国面临着失业率上升、高通胀和经济生产率下降。试图通过增加公共项目的公共支出（与凯恩斯主义的需求管理战略相一致）来提振经济产出似乎只会让事情变得更糟。结果，福利支出被视为政府和中产阶级再也负担不起的奢侈品。

英 国

1942年发布的《贝弗里奇报告》概述了支撑现代英国福利国家的基本原则。这份报告的正式名称为《社会保险及相关服务报告》，它将作为1945年至1951年工党政府的历史性福利国家计划一个总体的"主蓝图"。有人认为，这份历史性文件中包含的经济细节，是在与约翰·梅纳德·凯恩斯磋商后设计的。这有助于提高文件在议会中有影响力的政治家眼中的可信度。此外，该报告巩固了英国政府对其公民个人经济安全"国家最低标准"的保证。贝弗里奇勋爵坚持认为，基本的经济安全是公民权赋予的政治权利，同时对过度免费享用公共物品的潜在可能性和产生"福利依赖"文化的倾向表示担忧。因此，他坚持认为，公民有责任尽可能地自食其力。

贝弗里奇认为，政府不仅有责任，而且有能力通过向那些生计和收入能力受到结构性经济变化和危机破坏的人提供基本水平的公共支持来消除贫困。为了达到这些目的，《贝弗里奇报告》提出了五个"巨大的罪恶"，他声称在现代社会中，"没有一个民主国家能够为它的公民承受这些"："贫困、疾病、无知、肮脏和懒惰"。贝弗里奇认为，这五个弊病代表了对英国社会整体福祉的威胁。他坚持认为，为了民主社会的继续繁荣，必须根除它们。然而，贝弗里奇断言，政府需要采取适当的方式来消除这些社会弊病，既不能阻碍或扼杀个人的主动性，也不能鼓励对福利的依赖。贝弗里奇的许多观点（尽管不是全部）帮助塑造了现代英国福利国家的价值观和目标。虽然有些人声称，在大多数方案的细节中贝弗里奇的直接参与是相当有限的，但他的核心原则在指引政策制定者的方向方面的影响无可争辩。

在第二次世界大战后的几年里，政府通过了一项覆盖所有英国公民的普遍社会保险计划。在其综合框架下，工人从他们每周的工资中做出个人贡献，以换取广泛的社会保障。这些措施包括全民健康和医疗保险、失业保险、老年人养老金、生育补助、工伤保险和丧葬费用补助。在报告中提到的五大罪恶中，只有"贫困"这一条得到了直接解决。也就是说，这份报告有助于为后续立法的通过奠定基础，这些立法涵盖了"疾病、无知、肮脏和懒惰"等残余弊病。此外，该报告将"自由"的政治定义从"言论、写作和投票的自由"扩展到"免于贫困、疾病、无知、肮脏和懒惰"。也许最重要的是，《贝弗里奇报告》将人们的注意力引向了采用综合福利制度的重要性（见方框5）。

方框5　受《贝弗里奇报告》启发的主要立法措施

1945年　《家庭津贴法》

1946年　《国家保险法》

1946年　《国家保险（工伤）法》

1946年　《国民保健服务法》（1948年7月实施）

1947年　《城乡规划法》

1947年　《新城镇法》

1948年　《国家援助法》

1948年　《儿童法》

1949年　《住房法》

　　20世纪70年代，英国政府面临着国际金融冲击、高通胀和不断上升的失业率。工党政府最初用国家主导的需求管理战略来应对，但最终证明无效。1976年，英国经济恶化到需要国际货币基金组织（IMF）救助，以防止该国货币彻底崩溃。在接下来的几个月里，政府官员和公民都开始对维持目前福利国家的负担能力提出严肃的质疑，更普遍的是对政府在经济中的恰当作用和职能的质疑。1979年玛格丽特·撒切尔掌权时，她注意到，近70%的英国家庭至少有一名家庭成员获得了某种形式的现金福利。撒切尔的保守党政府决心削减社会福利支出，对国家公共部门发起了一场联合攻击。我们将在第五章对此进行更深入的探讨。

　　19世纪后期发展起来的行政系统，不足以解决工业化世界许多复杂的政治和公共问题。现代福利国家的演变反映了当代社会的动态性质。随着社会变得更加民主，公民对政府提供更多公共服务的要求越来越高（见表2）。为了满足日益复杂的社会不断增长的需求和期望，政府官僚机构和公共管理系统被迫扩大。20世纪80年代，中右翼和中左翼政党中的保守派政治运动，开始动员起来反对"大政府"及其孪生的再分配引擎——高税收和巨额赤字。

表2　1870—1980年部分年份的政府就业情况（占选定国家总就业人数的百分比）

国家	1870	1913	1937	1960	1980
德国	1.2	2.4	4.3	9.9	14.6
瑞典	2.2	3.5	4.7	12.8	30.3
英国	4.9	4.1	6.5	14.8	21.1
美国	2.9	3.7	6.8	14.7	15.1

资料来源：经济合作与发展组织（2015），"公共部门的就业情况"，《2000—2015年政府一览》，经济合作与发展组织出版社，巴黎。DOI: http: //dx. doi. org/10. 1787/gov_glance-2015-22-en；改编自马苏德·汉穆亚的《公共部门就业统计：方法、结构和趋势》（国际劳工组织统计局，日内瓦，1999）©国际劳工组织，1999。

第五章

"新公共管理"走向全球

20世纪70年代的一系列经济冲击,终结了所谓的凯恩斯主义国家的"黄金时代"。石油输出国组织(OPEC)领导的石油禁运导致世界原油价格飙升。随之而来的是高通胀和高失业率的结合("滞胀")。公司利润迅速蒸发,股价暴跌。同时,世界上的很多工业化国家政府无助地袖手旁观。一些"有事业心"的领导人面对大规模失业和强烈的社会绝望,看到了金融服务业的巨大增长潜力。在政府旨在放松金融市场管制的新举措推动下,并在电子交易和金融工具技术突破的帮助下,一个以全球金融为基础的资本主义(被称为"金融化")的新时代诞生了。如今,精明的投资者可以瞬间在全球自由转移数十亿美元,他们把自己的命运押在了那些政策能够确保在最短时间内获得最高回报的国家。因此,现代政府承受着巨大的压力,要"合理化"它们的税收制度,削减公共支出,以证明它们的"投资价值"。在这个过程中,许多公共产品将被掏空,以吸引新一代贪婪的全球投资者。

传统的行政层级制度被认为过于僵化和不灵活，无法适应全球化时代释放出来的充满活力的政治和经济力量。世界各地的高级公共管理者和公共领导人越来越多地期待一套新的以市场为导向的战略，希望提高官僚机构的效率，最大化纳税人的钱。一种新的"管理主义"强调私营部门的价值观，如"及时性"、"响应性"和"成本节约"，后来被称为"新公共管理"（NPM），开始在世界上一些主要的公共机构中扎根（方框6）。

方框6　新公共行政

虽然与新公共管理有着相似的首字母缩写，但"新公共行政"（NPA）是20世纪60年代出现的一种非常不同的管理范式。新公共行政将"公共服务"置于其管理信条的核心，它采用一套管理原则，强调"公民美德"和"公民赋权"的价值观。新公共行政与亚伯拉罕·马斯洛和他的"人本主义心理学"学派的同事们的开创性工作有关，新公共行政的倡导者认为，创建有助于其雇员身心健康的组织条件对行政生产率至关重要。20世纪60年代末，新公共行政学者德怀特·瓦尔多主持了一次历史性的会议，旨在促进一种崭新的治理公共管理"未来"的对话。为了探索创新的方法，瓦尔多邀请了一些该领域崭露头角的先驱参加。年轻而充满活力的与会者反对"种族歧视"、"社会不公正"和"不平等"，试图重新定位公共管理专业，摆脱对行政效率的"狭隘"追求，走向"民主平等"和"社会公正"。然而，也有批评新公共行政的人。一些主流公共管理学院的杰出人物表达了关切，他们主张用源于理想主义情绪的"软"知识取代"科学上可检验"的管理原则。

澳大利亚前财政部长迈克尔·基廷在《OECD预算杂志》2001年一篇题为"公共管理改革与经济和社会发展"的文章中，总结了他的国家在过去十五年中一直试图进行的新公共管理改革背后的力量。这些问题包括："1.税收水平、预算赤字和/或公共债务过高，如果不采取行动情况可能会变得更糟；2.政府方案往往无法实现其目标和/或不具备成本效益，因此它们不具有资金价值；3.行政机构不能充分满足客户的需要，包括部长本人；4.政府本身也是问题的一部分，因为它变得太大、太烦人了。"虽然多年来出现了对新公共管理不同的定义和解释，但著名的公共管理学者唐纳德·凯特尔概述了与新公共管理相关的绝大多数文献中似乎共有的六个核心特征："生产率、市场化、服务导向、权力下放、政策导向和问责制。"

第一波新公共管理政策出现在英国的玛格丽特·撒切尔（1979—1990）、美国的罗纳德·里根（1981—1989）、澳大利亚的马尔科姆·弗雷泽（1975—1983）和加拿大的布赖恩·马尔罗尼（1984—1993）等保守党政府的政治改革议程中。虽然玛格丽特·撒切尔首相的政府是20世纪70年代末首批正式采用以新公共管理为基础的方法的政府之一，但许多相关的原则很快被全球的各级政府所采用。一些最早的新公共管理应用可以在北加利福尼亚州的市区观察到，持续的经济衰退迫使城市领导者去寻找削减政府开支的创新方法。新西兰和澳大利亚政府也紧随其后，建立了它们自己的新公共管理的行政议程。不久，到20世纪80年代中期，大多数经合组织国家也将新公共管理引入其公共部门的组织中。

> **方框7　新自由主义**
>
> 　　新公共管理是一种治理范式，认同一套以市场为导向的原则，这些原则植根于被称为"新自由主义"的政治经济学理论。新自由主义最初是由一批政治上温和的经济学家和法律学者提出的，他们隶属于第一次世界大战后德国出现的"弗赖堡学派"。这个词后来被用作一个流行语，指的是由诺贝尔经济学奖得主米尔顿·弗里德曼和弗雷德里希·冯·哈耶克等经济学家领导的"回归市场"运动。新自由主义颂扬个人私利、经济效率和无节制竞争的功效，它是与福利国家紧缩和经济紧缩联系在一起的。在20世纪70年代，这种学说更极端的部分被称为新自由主义，被拉丁美洲暴虐的独裁者所采用，比如智利总统奥古斯托·皮诺切特，作为他们严厉的反社会运动的一部分。然而，在20世纪90年代，这个术语被左翼学者用来严厉批评美国的政策倡议，这些政策倡议的目的是在共产主义剧变后，将美国式的"牛仔资本主义"传播到东欧的前苏联集团国家。在过去的三十年里，基于新自由主义的新公共管理方案被不同的政治人物采用，强调私营部门的效率措施和绩效标准。一些最著名的人物包括美国的罗纳德·里根和比尔·克林

顿；英国的玛格丽特·撒切尔和托尼·布莱尔；加拿大的布赖恩·马尔罗尼；澳大利亚的马尔科姆·弗雷泽、罗伯特·霍克和保罗·基廷。

新公共管理基于一种被称为"新自由主义"的新兴学说，推崇自我调节的自由市场，将其视为公民治理的良性模式（见方框7）。因此，新公共管理将与传统的公共管理相关的看重"公平"和"公正"的原则与程序，从属于强调效率标准和生产率目标的以业务为导向的原则。这种向私营部门"管理主义"的转变迫使公共部门机构应用（或在许多情况下误用）基于规范的策略，如全面质量管理（TQM）、"精益六西格玛"和"目标管理"。在管理主义的逻辑下，"公务员"被转变为公共部门的"服务提供者"，其目的被重新定位于满足顾客的需求。

第一波新公共管理浪潮

罗纳德·里根总统在1981年宣誓就职时，公布了他新的经济复苏计划。总统备受争议的计划，即减轻美国最高收入人群的税收负担，将成为他的被称为"里根经济学"的经济议程的基石。作为对公共部门更广泛意识形态攻击的组成部分，"里根经济学"包括大幅削减一系列政府社会福利项目。为了追求更小、更少"障碍"的政府，里根采纳了一系列受新公共管理启发的"权力下放"改革措施，旨在将联邦监管权力转移到州和地方行政单位。在这个被称为"新联邦主义"的倡议下，许多新的行政责任现在将由各州承担——通常很少得到国家政府的财政援助。

里根依赖于一种被称为"整体拨款"的预算工具,将许多社会项目的财政责任和管理——从学校午餐计划到医疗补助——下放到各州。虽然社会保障等主要福利项目将继续由联邦政府管理和监督,但这位保守派总统试图在美国的医疗保险系统中引入精益凭证系统,以鼓励"竞争"和"效率"。里根的努力虽然最终没有成功,但它代表了一种前所未有的举措,即在实施一项重大的社会服务计划的行政过程中引入私营部门的原则。

里根的新联邦主义议程深深植根于缩小政府规模的意识形态承诺中。这也是经济学的"公共选择"学派所宣扬的学说。该学派主张公民个人"用脚投票",认为地方政府更关心他们"客户"的需求。此外,他们认为,分散的、精简的行政治理形式不太可能通过"不必要的"法规来"阻碍"私营部门的生产率。公共选择学派寻求将保护个人选择和私人主动性作为最高的社会优先权,坚持使用严格的"经济"原则和工具来评估特定社会项目上花费纳税人"辛苦挣来的"钱的"价值"。

"里根经济学"深受作为总统主要经济顾问之一的威廉·A.尼斯卡宁的影响。尼斯卡宁是诺贝尔经济学奖得主米尔顿·弗里德曼的学生,他的1971年极具影响力的著作《官僚主义和代议制政府》激发了全球的新公共管理运动。尼斯卡宁认为,"理性的"公共部门官僚和立法机构领导人会想方设法以牺牲纳税人和社会效率为代价来扩大自己的范围和权力。尼斯卡宁断言,政客们往往在政治上受欢迎的计划上超支,以争取更多的选票;负责执行这些方案的公共管理者一直在寻找方法扩大其政府机构的规模和范围。尼斯卡宁合乎逻辑地得出结论,即使在公职人员能够找到以更少经济资源履行其职责和职能的情况下,他们也没有什么激励这样做。相反,公共管理者总是寻求"最大化"由有政治头脑的立法者分配给他们的预算。

里根总统在尼斯卡宁观点的深刻影响下,签署了《12291号行政令》,要求公共机构使用成本效益分析来评估所有涉及监管和社会支出的提案。在这个命令下,许多负责行政监督与执行的社会方案和公共机构的预算要么被大幅度削减,要么被完全取消。事实上,使用这些方法大大削弱了像环境保护署(EPA)这样的政府组织所行使的监管权力。

虽然英国首相玛格丽特·撒切尔和里根一样蔑视"大政府",但她并不赞同里根的新联邦主义所强调的权力下放和赋予地方政府权力。事实上,撒切尔认为地方公共管理者效率低下,容易滋生政治腐败。因此,撒切尔试图用新的"人头税"或"社区费"取代传统的地方税率,以严格限制地方议会的收入。后来,撒切尔首相在强大的政治压力下推翻了这个不得人心的决定。

撒切尔厌恶政府的扩张,她认为这与"无法控制的"公共支出率有关,她强烈谴责对私人财富征税以资助"低效的"政府管理项目和政策的做法。撒切尔的公共部门紧缩运动的核心是其有争议的"中期财政战略"(MTFS)。中期财政战略将把英国的财政和支出大臣的关注点,从短期的税收和支出计划转向旨在限制英国货币增长的长期战略举措。中期财政战略规定的严格支出限制,自然给公共决策者和公共管理者带来了新的挑战。为了证明自己的立场是正确的,这位激发争论的首相竭尽全力让她的同僚相信,为了社会的"更大利益",她的紧缩的、基于新公共管理的公共部门裁员运动是有好处的。为了说明她提出削减开支的理由,撒切尔将尼斯卡宁关于官僚主义的书列为所有高级内阁成员的"必读书"。在议会中一群狂热的党内忠诚分子（被称为撒切尔主义者）的支持下，这位极端保守的领导人持续进行一场轰轰烈烈的改革运动，以建立一个丰富的基于新公共管理的改革，其中包括大幅减少政府法规和国有企业私有化。

撒切尔认为，支配着英国庞大的公务员官僚机构的管理和领导结构已经变得呆滞和不灵活。为了启动她的革命性的、基于新公共管理的效率和服务改革的实施，撒切尔采取了一项全面的行政计划，要求公共"管理者"承担起更有效地"管理"其组织的责任。根据一项被称为"下一步"的新自由主义方案，各种公共服务将通过类似市场的安排提供，并由拥有行政权力和履行授权所需资源的管理者进行监督。以前由各政府部门执行的具体服务任务和职能，现在将被重新分配到独立运行的单一功能导向的机构和组织。在这一创新的行政框架下，大臣们仍然负责制定公共政策，而涉及执行的管理职能和责任则由独立机构来管理。由于在严格的"类似私营部门"的责任标准下运作，机构管理者的业绩水平受到其相关内阁部门负责人的密切监督。

作为她更广泛的新公共管理议程的一部分，撒切尔监督了大量国有企业向私营企业和投资者的出售。她的众所周知的私有化运动始于20世纪80年代初，当时出售了英国航空航天公司、英国铁路公司和相关的英国港口公司等知名行业巨头，后来继续推进罗尔斯-罗伊斯飞机发动机公司和英国石油公司等的私有化。在许多情况下，国有企业被以低于市场价值的价格出售。这样做的部分原因是基于这样一种假设，即它们的新经理将利用剩余资金来更新工厂设施，使其具有全球竞争力。玛格丽特·撒切尔的继任者约翰·梅杰后来将一些"下一步"机构私有化,并扩大了其他各种公共服务外包的做法。

撒切尔政府认为,地方委员会的管理者在英国公共住房部门的建设和管理上存在严重失误,因此安排了大量政府所有房产的私人出售。以前,这些委员会保留了对数百万财产的行政控制权,完全不受基本法律准则或程序责任的约束。为了提高住房管理的行政效率,撒切尔首相颁布了1980年的《住房法》。根据这项措施,有经济能力的长期租户拥有"购买权"的选择权,并通过重要的法律规定以确保这些租赁"客户"的财产权。[69]不幸的是,撒切尔善意的"改革"执行不力。在没有任何全面的公共补贴融资计划的情况下,许多租户无力购买他们新"私有化"的房屋。结果,他们被迫搬到更便宜、往往更不理想的社区,从而加剧了英国社会阶层之间的既有差距。

类似地,当面临英国工业部门衰退导致的大规模结构性失业时,撒切尔将她坚定不移的信任交给"自由市场"来决定哪些职业将受到保护或被废除。撒切尔相信,英国的经济未来掌握在金融服务部门手中,她的政府采取了一系列政策,帮助加速了伦敦"金融城"作为全球领先贸易中心的重生。作为这种"转变"的一部分,撒切尔首相对公共部门控制的煤矿、矿井和制造厂实施了严格的、基于新公共管理的私营部门绩效标准。出于对新公共管理原则的忠诚,撒切尔要求清晰地列出目标和目的,并根据严格的效率标准评估产出。

在削减国家支出的强烈愿望的驱使下,撒切尔将注意力集中在与英国国家福利部门相关的低效问题上。其中最引人注目和最有争议的是,她高调发起了改革儿童福利补助的运动,该补助已普遍提供给所有工作的母亲,无论其收入和财富如何。撒切尔坚持认为,社会保障和儿童福利计划应该只向"真正需要的人"开放,她试图实施严格的经济状况调查,以减轻国家纳税人的财政负担。尽管首相以其不妥协的精神而闻名,但面对选民甚至她自己政党的一些成员的强烈政治反弹,她被迫缩减了这些改革。

这位"铁娘子"没有被吓倒,继续努力改革英国"过时的"公共养老金制度。撒切尔试图将员工账户从工会的控制中"解放"出来,允许员工在跳槽时随身携带他们的投资。撒切尔认为,消除将雇员养老金与现有雇主捆绑在一起的僵化的国家强加的障碍,将有助于鼓励雇员寻求更高技能和更高薪酬的职位。由于再次面临来自敌对政治选民的强大政治阻力,撒切尔被迫弱化了她的改革雄心。然而,这位果断的首相最终成功地对既有的财富调查资格要求实施了一些新公共管理式的行政改进。最终,她的政府得以在精简规则和程序方面取得长足进步,促进了利益分配的一致性和公平性。

撒切尔断言,与英国国民医疗服务(NHS)相关的所有问题的根源是结构性的官僚低效,而不是缺乏适当的资金,她从自由市场中寻找创新的解决方案。这位首相对基于新公共管理的解决方案的信念没有丝毫动摇,她授权公立医院领域向私营医疗服务提供商招标。本着这种精神,撒切尔政府制定了"灵活的"改革立法,通过将许多公共卫生服务外包给私营部门,赋予地方卫生当局更大的行政权力和权威,以帮助管理不断上涨的医疗费用。当她所在的保守党内部出现反对她推行的紧缩的经济改革和基于新自由主义的新公共管理计划的声音时,撒切尔公然宣称:"你们想转向就转向吧。我是不会转向的。"

澳大利亚

澳大利亚运用受新公共管理启发的"管理主义"思想和实践所进行的实验,与其美国和英国的同伴没有什么不同。事实上,有文件证明,澳大利亚公共服务委员会的官员和行政人员深受撒切尔和里根政府进行的新公共管理实验的启发。作为澳大利亚联邦政府的公共管理部门,澳大利亚公共服务委员会基于新公共管理的公共部门改革分三个阶段展开。最初,1983年的罗伯特·霍克总理和1996年的保罗·基廷总理的左倾澳大利亚工党政府(ALPG)向公众介绍了新公共管理计划,后来,这一计划被约翰·霍华德总理的保守的自由党-国家党联合政府更加严格地采纳。

20世纪80年代初,澳大利亚人生活艰难。事实证明,控制财政管理的凯恩斯主义行政框架,已无法为澳大利亚领导人提供令人满意的解决方案以应对该国日益加重的经济危机。作为一名前工会领导人,霍克总理承受着巨大的政治压力,要为他的工人提供救济和保证。在霍克的财政部长保罗·基廷的领导下,一批精挑细选的技术娴熟的文职行政人员,即所谓的官员,被邀请帮助制订新自由主义宏观经济政策方案。其重要特征包括:引入有利于企业的税收制度,并削减一系列公共支出,以应对通胀和政府债务。这位务实的总理还跨越意识形态的界限,向工会和私营企业寻求帮助,以实施一系列关键的新公共管理改革,解决该国陷入困境的工业部门生产率不断下降的问题。此外,这一改革举措的特点是大胆的放松管制和私有化运动,这将有助于该国的"政府商业企业"(GBE)部门发生巨大变化。

20世纪80年代中期,财政管理改进方案(FMIP)引入了一个新的框架,它是澳大利亚公共部门中新公共管理"制度化"的关键组成部分。财政管理改进方案是一个全面的战略管理方案,旨在解决许多公共服务委员会的机构之间程序操作中存在的"严重"系统效率低下问题,采用"基于结果"的原则来提高组织绩效。根据这些规定,公共管理者现在被"激励"去采取新的措施,简化从组织规划和预算预测到方案实施和评估的整个业务流程。

许多澳大利亚公共服务委员会改革的具体目标是改善国家和州政府之间的行政协调。作为这一努力的一部分,执行中更大的行政自主权和问责制被移交给地方当局。从财政和人力资源管理到政府商业企业的私有化,都采取了许多引人注目的新公共管理举措。基廷一上台就采取了一项全面的新公共管理计划,旨在重组该国过时的政府商业企业监管政策,使它们能够在全球范围内竞争。政府商业企业对该国国内生产总值的贡献超过10%,在澳大利亚经济中发挥着重要作用。例如,铁路、电力、天然气和供水等公共事业加在一起占了该国生产财富的近5%。同样令人印象深刻的是,作为一个整体,政府商业企业对该国私营企业股票的贡献接近40%。澳大利亚一些领先的政府商业企业包括著名的服务业巨头,如澳大利亚电信公司和雪山水力发电管理局,提供从电信到水力发电的基本服务。基廷采用了私营部门的客户服务方法,如"商业化",以改善服务的提供。新公共管理改革进程的下一个阶段被称为"公司化",在这一阶段,政府当局逐渐将某些政府商业企业的运营控制权移交给私人管理者。新公共管理演变的最后阶段涉及"私有化",即出售政府商业企业给私人。众所周知的例子包括国际企业品牌,如澳洲航空公司和联邦银行。

澳大利亚历届政府尝试的新公共管理改革，并没有充分解决澳大利亚公共部门长期以来根深蒂固的深层结构问题。批评者指出，澳大利亚公共服务委员会的财政管理改进方案的改革框架走得不够远，充其量不过是"一系列互不关联的管理思想和流程的仓库"。澳大利亚公共服务系统需要彻底改革，真正整合联邦和国家以下各级政府不同的管理职能，以改善机构间的协调。

第二次新公共管理浪潮

新公共管理的"第二次浪潮"最明显的标志是美国的比尔·克林顿和英国的托尼·布莱尔的政策议程。他们的新自由主义议程采用了里根和撒切尔时期的许多相同原则，但包括几项基于社会正义的倡议，即全面的从福利到工作的改革战略、新的最低工资政策，以及扩大对贫困工人及其家庭的减税计划。

1993年1月，美国总统比尔·克林顿一上台，就宣布他的政府坚决致力于财政稳定。这位新总统意识到，不受控制的公共支出可能会给不断上升的通货膨胀带来压力，他制定了对政府部门支出的明确预算限制。为了实现这些目标，克林顿政府寻求新的方法来创建一个"更精简"和更有效的公共部门。因此，这位温和的左翼总统采纳了一项被称为"政府再造"的新公共管理议程。这种方法的主要支持者特德·盖布勒和戴维·奥斯本试图推动一种新型的"催化型政府"，在这种政府中，政府官员应该"掌舵"政策议程，但多样化的公共和私营机构将参与实际的"划船"，或公共服务和项目的日常实施与交付。盖布勒和奥斯本的"催化型政府"的十大原则，强调了一个竞争型的和结果导向型的公共管理体系。

克林顿政府的"政府再造国家伙伴关系"包括实施国家绩效审查，用于减少政府浪费，提高行政效率，并确保加强官僚问责制。同样，布莱尔政府通过了全面支出审查和公共服务协议，以促进财政部和内阁各支出部门之间的更大协调，努力找到最有效的资源利用方式。此外，两国政府都采取了全面预算战略，确定长期支出的目标。

第二波新公共管理政策的成功实施，需要在各级政府和私营企业部门内运作的各种机构与行动者之间进行大量的协调和互动。不幸的是，在设计和实施这些政策战略时，往往没有考虑到这些复杂性，从而导致了管理噩梦的出现（方框8）。

克林顿为了解除对"过时的监管政策"阻碍创业的担忧，实施了一系列放松监管的措施，以便为金融服务部门提供更大的灵活性和自主权，使其能够自由利用全球市场中出现的新金融机会。例如，这些措施包括拆除许多分隔商业银行业务和投资银行业务，以及保险和证券公司分业经营的法律壁垒。然而，与这种放松管制相关的毁灭性风险，直到2008—2009年世界金融和房地产市场灾难性的崩溃才被充分认识到。

为了解决从"旧的"以制造业为基础的经济向"新的以金融为基础的经济"转型所带来的结构性失业和财务困难，克林顿寻求新公共管理战略来促进现代化、高技能、灵活的劳动力市场。克林顿的"工作福利"品牌，旨在创新性地将劳动技能发展培训与对失业者的公共援助结合起来，而不会让他们陷入"福利依赖"。据记载，克林顿的"从福利到工作"计划部分受到了罗纳德·里根1988年《家庭支持法案》的启发。克林顿从自己党内日益壮大的新自由主义运动中培养了其议程的政治支持者，

> **方框8　新公共管理的新自由主义：十项政府目标**
>
> 1. 催化型政府：掌舵，而非划船
> 2. 社区拥有型政府：授权，而不是服务
> 3. 竞争型政府：将竞争注入服务
> 4. 使命驱动型政府：转变规则驱动型组织
> 5. 结果导向型政府：资助成果，而不是投入
> 6. 客户驱动型政府：满足客户的需要，而不是官僚机构
> 7. 进取型政府：挣钱，而不是花钱
> 8. 预期型政府：预防，而不是治疗
> 9. 分权型政府：从层级制度到参与和团队合作
> 10. 市场导向型政府：通过市场推动变革
>
> 资料来源：戴维·奥斯本和特德·盖布勒，"政府再造（1992）"，引自罗伯特·B. 登哈特，《公共组织理论》，第5版，第145—146页

并被贴上了"新民主党"的标签。这些支持者包括新型的温和左派政治家，如阿尔·戈尔、戴夫·麦考迪、埃德·基尔戈尔和约瑟夫·利伯曼，克林顿希望将其政党对"集体福利"的传统承诺与新公共管理的"个人责任"和"问责制"原则结合起来。克林顿总统支持1996年《福利改革法案》，把它作为更广泛的新公共管理计划的一部分，该计划取代了罗斯福总统在20世纪30年代设立的受抚养子女家庭援助计划。克林顿政府的"政府再造"主导的"工作福利"计划，现在要求以"工作"换取福利。根据其严格的规定，领取者在被要求获得有报酬的就业或参加新的工作培训方案之前，最多只能领取两年的援助。累计援助五年

后，接受者的福利将被终止。这项政策允许公共管理者为儿童保育和医疗保险做出特别规定，以支持短期失业的母亲。然而，限制福利支付期限的严格规定，使得单身母亲很难参加必要的学校教育，而这是她们获得高薪工作的必要条件。

克林顿的"政府再造"倡议很像里根政府的新公共管理计划，许多由县和市政当局管理的社会服务外包给私营公司。在许多情况下，这阻碍了基本支持服务的提供，如为单收入的母亲提供儿童保育援助。在这些情况下，公共行政当局和私营实体之间往往缺乏复杂的协调，以便成功地实施这些政策和方案。我们将在第六章中探讨一些涉及政府间关系的主要实施问题。

首相托尼·布莱尔和后来的戈登·布朗领导的中间偏左的政府，决心创造一个只有"富人和游艇"的经济，采取了一些有史以来最引人注目和政治上最受欢迎的新自由主义计划。为了实现他的"新英国"愿景，布莱尔明白，他必须争取新的全球投资者群体。这将包括改变英国公共部门"做生意"的方式。布莱尔吸取了前任失败的教训，通过与财政部（和其他支出部门）、内阁委员会、特别工作组、商业团体和其他许多部门的紧密合作，实施了重要的新公共管理改革。作为这项努力的一部分，成立了三百多个工作队，向大臣们提供咨询和支持，以促进中央政府各部门之间的合作。与新公共管理的处方一致，财政部开始发布预算前报告或"绿色预算"，以便促进更高的透明度和问责制。此外，具有赤字意识的布莱尔首相和他的内阁推出了《财政稳定准则》，该准则强调健全财政管理的五项原则："透明"、"稳定"、"责任"、"公平"和"效率"。此外，该准则要求政府遵守明确规定的目标和规则。布莱尔政府坚定不移地致力于健全的财政管理，这让内阁大臣们接受了定期全面支出审查（CSR）制度。这些全面支出审查提供了根据严格的成本收益计算制定的明确的部门支出计划和目标。随后建立了"全面支出审查"和"公共服务协议"，以评估最有效的使用，努力消除浪费和低效率。此外，还设立了一个"绩效创新部门"，以确保政策设计和执行的更高一致性。

布莱尔政府为了限制"过度的"公共借贷倾向，还实施了众所周知的"黄金法则"，即将公共债务严格限制在不超过国内生产总值的40%。因此，布莱尔保证他的政府不会在医疗、教育或社会保障方面进一步赤字开支。布莱尔的福利改革方案包括一个新的"从福利到工作"的计划，该计划直接模仿克林顿版的"工作福利"。布莱尔基于培训的福利改革实验最初通过对私有化设施收取一次性"暴利税"进行融资，与他对"社会公正"的公开承诺以及他的选举承诺相一致，即根据确保个人"责任"和"义务"的新标准分配福利。

总而言之，布莱尔的社会政策改革议程集中在三个基本领域：（1）失业福利，（2）对贫困劳动者的补贴，（3）国民医疗服务体系（NHS）。布莱尔的新举措主要是受撒切尔基于新公共管理的福利国家大胆改革的启发，着眼于精简行政职能和程序，以提高效率。这些部门颁布了新的问责制和透明度措施，以确保改革成功。遵循撒切尔的推理路线，布莱尔认为，仅仅提供"更多的钱"不足以解决英国病态福利体系中更深层次的结构性问题。因此，这位新自由主义首相寻求用一个更"灵活的"工作福利培训计划取代英国的"家长式"福利制度，这与私营组织的新公共管理"伙伴关系"模式相一致。

新公共管理的第一次浪潮起源于对凯恩斯主义"大政府"的强烈反对,在里根和撒切尔政府中获得了极大的支持。在短短的几年里,似乎出现了一个大流行:新公共管理的思想已经控制了世界各国政府。然而,正如我们所看到的,不同国家的不同领导人强调了新公共管理方法的不同方面。将它们联系在一起的共同主线是,它们都强调提高"效率"和实施基于绩效的问责标准和实践。具有讽刺意味的是,在某些情况下,需要更强(而不是更弱)的政府干预,以便在这些国家的各级管理机构和程序中将这种基于市场的模式制度化。值得注意的是,20世纪70年代澳大利亚以及90年代美国和英国的民主左翼政府,都曾大力推行一些最引人注目的新公共管理政策。今天,在几乎所有涉及公共部门的组织使命声明和政治对话中,都能明显见到新公共管理对客户服务、目标管理以及基于量化的绩效和责任标准的重视。事实上,毫无疑问,现在各级政府都采纳了新公共管理原则,这表明这种管理方式无可替代。但是没有其他的选择吗?近年来出现的公共管理中的新运动一直在挑战这一观点。

第六章

新行政时代

从"最佳实践"到"反思实践"

正如我们在第五章中看到的,许多政府都进行了重要的新公共管理改革,其重点是建立私营企业式的绩效和责任标准,以促进效率和提升组织绩效的名义采用了许多定量的绩效标准。然而,由于只是关注所谓的"底线",这些方法中的许多都未能解决导致绩效不佳的深层系统或结构问题。因此,在过去几十年里,各种替代方法和途径在公共管理专业和实践中日益流行。例如,由唐纳德·舍恩和其他人引入的反思实践已经在组织管理领域获得了坚实的立足点。反思实践取决于对一个经理的自我评估,即"做对了什么,他/她可能做错了什么,以及他/她在哪些方面可以做得更好"。组织成员边做边学,这样他们就可以实时改进现有的实践和方法。然而,只有最高层的组织领导才有权力在他们各自的机构内创造一种"边做边学"的文化。这意味着员工必须获得组织内的领导者和管理者赋予的自主权和灵活性,以便去承担风险和进行实验。

表3 学习型组织的特征

	支持创新	不支持创新/压制创新
目的	利益相关者、社会利益、不断学习	主要的财务利益
目标	组织的	狭义职能的
结构	异质结构、跨职能的适应性互动	层级严格的职能报告
内部关系	协作、跨职能的	竞争的
奖励、认可	非竞争的,赞扬组织的成就	零和竞争、专注个人,基于执行任务和实现目标
失败的处理	被视为学习的机会,重视了解什么是行不通的,明智的风险承担文化	惩罚、批评
成功的处理	团队合作得到认可,对更大利益的贡献得到赞扬	归因于个人
时间范围	长期和短期	仅有短期
投资评估依据	考虑潜在的市场、客户、竞争对手以及财务评估	只用通常的金融工具
探索思想	广泛寻找新技术和工序	仅限于行业内竞争公认的研究
实验	鼓励并支持教育和培训,提供时间和辅导	不被认为是有价值的实践

资料来源:吉普西·B. 兰尼,2014年6月20日在加利福尼亚州立大学北岭分校举行的In2In网络论坛会议上关于"21世纪戴明的思想"的幻灯片演示

创建了所谓的"学习型组织"文化的领导者,通常会鼓励员工对他们做出的决策和采取的行动所产生的积极与消极的反馈进行反思。此外,这类组织中的冲突和困境是通过管理者及其

下属之间坦诚的讨论来解决的。领导和创新专家吉普西·B.兰尼确定了学习型组织的一些关键特征，如表3所示。

"新经济学"与系统学习

威廉·爱德华兹·戴明在他广为流传的著作《工业、政府和教育的新经济学》的最后一句断言，过度强调"符合规范、零缺陷、六西格玛质量标准和其他基于规范的妙策"的管理过程"都没有抓住要点"。乍看之下，戴明仔细斟酌的评论似乎是对新公共管理的量化绩效措施的严厉谴责。然而，情况肯定不是这样。相反，戴明试图将管理层狭隘强调绩效技术指标，重新定位到采用更广泛的领导哲学的重要性上。戴明解释说，效率意味着做"正确的"事情。他接着说，而高效的领导"从一开始就做正确的事情"。因此，戴明坚持认为，领导者必须拥有清晰的愿景，并能够有效地将他的愿景传达给组织中的其他成员。

戴明根据没有一个机构是完全孤立运作的这一信念，断言运转良好的组织的特点是作为服务于共同目的的整体"系统"的一部分履行它们的任务和职责。相比之下，传统的组织文化侧重于改进系统的各个部分（即单个机构和其中的部门），而不是侧重于机构在与其他组织相互依赖的系统中的功能。在戴明看来，"一个系统是一个由相互依赖的组件组成的网络"，这些组件协调一致地工作，以完成由组织领导人勾勒和支持的特定目标。为了说明这一点，戴明将组织中的管理者比作管弦乐队的指挥。在戴明的解释中，指挥的角色是让单个音乐家作为更大的交响乐的一部分来演奏。如果最有才华的小提琴手不能与管弦乐队的其他成员同步，演奏就会失败。事实上，为了取得成功，音乐家们必须以一种相互依赖的方式工作，每一名成员都要支持其他人，反之亦然。为了帮助我们更好地理解领导力在塑造一个促进信任与合作而不是破坏它们的系统中的重要性，戴明概述了他著名的高效组织的"十四点"，这些在方框9中可以看到。

公共管理者如果不能正确理解他们的工作如何与其他机构履行的职能相互依存，可能会产生灾难性的后果。为了说明这一点，让我们简要地看一个与儿童福利和安全有关的引人注目的案例。在洛杉矶县，儿童福利的管理依赖于多个县机构和无数管理者的复杂互动和共同参与。家庭和儿童服务部（DCFS）、心理健康部、社会服务部、地方学区、县治安部以及地区检察官办公室和家庭法院，共同参与评估被置于县监管下的儿童的福祉。虽然这些机构（以及其中的各个部门）在这一评估和保护过程中履行着许多相互关联的重要职能，但它们在履行自己的职责时却常常显得互不相关。

> **方框9　威廉·爱德华兹·戴明关于高效组织的"十四点"**
>
> 1. 建立改善服务的永恒目标。
> 2. 管理层必须承担变革的领导责任。
> 3. 消除对大规模检查的需求；首先将质量构建在流程中。
> 4. 最小化总成本。任何一种物品或服务都转向单一供应商；建立忠诚和信任的长期关系。
> 5. 专注于系统的持续改进将导致成本的持续降低。
> 6. 建立一个持续的"在职培训"项目。
> 7. 管理的目标应该是支持下属把工作做得更好。

8. 消除恐惧感,让每个人都可以高效地为组织工作。
9. 打破部门之间的壁垒,帮助他们作为一个团队工作。
10. 消除目标管理和其他数字目标。生产率低下的原因归于体制,因此超出了员工的能力范围。
11. 消除那些让员工丧失以服务为荣的权利的障碍。
12. 消除那些让经理们丧失以服务为荣的权利的障碍。
13. 建立一个积极的教育和自我完善计划。
14. 让组织中的每个人都参与进来,共同完成转型。

资料来源:改编自威廉·爱德华兹·戴明研究所和威廉·爱德华兹·戴明的《走出危机》86

在最极端的情况下,各机构之间未能协调和共享信息可能是致命的。2009年到2013年间,有三名儿童在洛杉矶儿童福利系统的监管下死亡。同样令人担忧的是,由该县任命的负责调查这些悲惨死亡背后原因的蓝带委员会发现,已经报告的其他几十起虐待儿童的案件并没有得到有关机构的适当调查。该委员会的报告给出的理由是机构间沟通和协调不佳,表明这一悲剧是全系统的漏报造成的。这些儿童福利案件中有许多是在本应相互协调的机构之间"被遗漏"的。在委员会的报告发布后,洛杉矶县家庭和儿童服务部机构负责人证实:"该县面临许多挑战,没有一个机构可以完全负责儿童保护……身心健康、家庭和儿童服务部、观察和执法以及一大堆其他组织,包括私营组织,都必须对儿童保护负责。"

从刚才令人心碎的例子中我们可以看出,沟通对于机构间合作至关重要。然而,为了在不同机构运作的公共管理者之间进行真正的交流,他们必须对各自的职责和职能如何相互联系有一个共同的认识。然而在现实中,跨县、跨地区和跨州司法管辖的公共部门组织之间的对话很少。封闭的组织文化常常使管理者看不到他们各自的职能和职责是如何依赖于机构外其他人的工作的。事实上,大多数传统的自上而下的命令和控制的组织文化都有不利的"盲点",这可能阻碍他们的领导者和管理者将他们的许多问题、威胁、机遇、财政资源视为共同的现象(在这些案例中它们可能实际存在)。

虽然机构间合作的好处应该是显而易见的,但培育促进不同公共机构之间沟通和持续对话的途径并非易事。也就是说,机构间的联系最容易通过其雇员的个人和专业互动来促进。例如,当来自不同机构的员工通过共同的教育和培训经历相互交流时,可以建立许多深厚而持久的职业纽带。为了更深入地研究这一过程是如何工作的,让我们看一个案例,一群来自不同组织的受管理约束的雇员分享共同的研究生专业教育。

几年前,洛杉矶县首席行政官发起了一项倡议,探索一种开发创新培训和基于学位课程的途径,为处于职业生涯中期的县雇员提供所需的基本技能,以应对公共机构面临的新挑战。由于这些讨论,该县开始与当地一所大学合作,通过"学生群"的学习模式在各县机构现场提供研究生学位和培训课程。参加该大学公共管理硕士学位(MPA)的县雇员将一起参加为期两年的相同课程。通过密集的课堂讨论和小组互动,小组成员逐渐敏锐地意识到他们自己的工作是如何与其组织部门和机构之外的其他人的工作相互依存的。也许最重要的是,学生们参与了实质性的讨论,讨论内容涉及如何应用他们在课堂上分享的学术和实践组织知识，以改善他们自己机构之间的沟通和协调。

新公共服务

在研究了系统思维如何在理论和实践中发挥作用之后，让我们来看看另一种近年来越来越受关注的新兴公共管理方法。21世纪初出现了一种被称为"新公共服务"（NPS）的新范式，它起源于与新公共管理方法核心原则有关的一个如何看待政府和公共部门的主要目的的基本哲学争论。新公共服务的主要支持者珍妮特·V. 登哈特和罗伯特·B. 登哈特为了寻求解决一些核心问题，如"关于公共服务的性质、行政在治理中的作用，以及围绕官僚主义、效率、响应能力和问责制的价值观冲突"，他们强调以公民为导向的美德高于商业的原则。他们认为，治理首先需要专注于创造"公共价值"，这一术语最早是由哈佛大学肯尼迪政府学院的管理学教授马克·H. 摩尔提出的。在过去的二十年里，新公共服务对创造公共价值的重视，在公共管理的专业研究和实践中日益受到关注。创造公共价值包括鼓励公民更直接地参与建立集体目标，然后与公民一起制定实现这些目标的策略。根据管理专家约翰·布赖森的说法，这意味着"生产企业、政策、计划、项目、服务，或者物质、技术、社会、政治和文化基础设施要促进公共利益和生产价格合理的公共品"。

公共管理者有责任开发创新方法，以建立公民对其公共机构的更大信任。在这一努力中，公共管理者必须提出几个基本问题。这些问题包括：该组织最初创建的目的是什么？为什么会继续存在？它为谁服务？我们如何知道这个组织是否成功地

实现了由公民和为公民服务的公共部门组织合作确立的公共价值观和相关政策目标？（见方框10）

> **方框10　新公共服务的核心原则**
>
> 1. 公务员的作用是帮助公民实现他们的共同利益，而不是引导社会走向新的方向。
> 2. 通过集体努力、协作进程和共同领导，可以最有效地满足公共需求。
> 3. 公共利益是关于共同价值观对话的结果，而不是个人私利的聚集。
> 4. 公务员不应该仅仅回应顾客的要求，而是应该在公民信任的基础上建立关系。
> 5. 公务员必须遵守法律和宪法、社区价值观、政治规范、职业标准和公民利益。
>
> 资料来源：罗伯特·B. 登哈特、珍妮特·V. 登哈特和玛丽亚·P. 阿里斯蒂格塔，《公共和非营利组织中的人类行为管理》，第467—470页

珍妮特和罗伯特采用了"服务而不是驾驶"这一时髦用语，试图以"民主问责"和"公民参与"等价值观取代新公共管理的相当狭隘地只关注"效率"（以及与之相关的概念）。新公共服务的前提是相信，让公民更多地参与政治-政策程序，并从一开始就让他们在这些程序的形成中有真正的发言权，将有助于他们亲自投入到自己社区有创造意义的建设中。通过一个被称为"协商治理"的过程，政策和行政决策是通过与政府官员、政策专家、商业人士、媒体和其他相关利益群体处于同一水平的公民进

行讨论，建立共识达成的。在新公共服务的治理模式下，公民被视为"利益相关者"，他们积极参与界定问题，并帮助制订反映他们所居住社区的独特条件和特征的解决方案。新公共服务强调民主价值和参与治理的重要性，它在许多方面与我们在第五章提到的德怀特·瓦尔多的新公共行政方法高度一致。

　　一个用来促进和帮助组织这种涉及众多利益相关者讨论的工具，是一个被称为"战略规划周期"（有时称为"战略变化周期"）的审议过程。战略规划周期是一种更开放，通常更具包容性的战略规划模式，特别适合在公共和非营利部门使用。与传统的自上而下的战略规划方法相比，战略规划周期的结构往往是更加有组织的和不拘一格的，对于帮助公共管理者监督不同的利益相关者怎样及何时可以参与多阶段的审议规划过程特别有用。作为这个过程的一部分，利益相关者分析通常被用来帮助参与者更好地理解组织周围的政治、社会和经济环境。更好地理解公共组织在更广泛系统中的定位，将非常有助于公共管理者确定他们及其委托人面临的重要战略问题。这些公共管理者可以运用前面讨论过的反思实践原则，利用这一重要信息来改进他们做出的决策和随后的行动。

　　随着公共管理者转变为"人民"和政府机构之间的促进者和诚实中间人的新角色，他们必须在设计和实施日益复杂的全球问题解决方案时，学会与不同的公民群体建立非传统的伙伴关系。与此同时，新公共服务模式的成功取决于有能力参与深入政策辩论的见多识广的公民的积极参与。仅仅让公民有更多机会参与治理过程是不够的；公民必须熟悉社会面临的重要政治问题，以及与其相关的政策和行政程序。

然而,新公共服务的批评者指出,美国大多数非专业公民不具备公共政策(及其相关过程)的知识,或以创造"公共价值"的方式成功开展"公共工作"所需的专业管理技能。根据备受推崇的《经济学人》杂志的民主指数,一些国家比其他国家更适合新公共服务的参与式治理形式。该指数由经济学人信息部编制,采用60个独立指标对160多个国家的民主状况进行排名。这个指标考虑了属于一般类别的广泛因素,这些因素包括:(1)选举过程,(2)公民自由,(3)政府运作,(4)政治参与,(5)政治文化。该指数是同类指标中最全面的衡量之一。根据该指数,挪威、瑞典和冰岛等国家在成功运作新公共服务治理过程所需的素质方面可能表现得更好,而排名靠后的国家,如美国,或许不太可能做到这一点。

这些批评者继续指出,即使一个特定的国家拥有"正确的"因素组合,使其成为新公共服务的成熟候选者,这仍然给我们留下了悬而未决的问题,即"创造公共价值"首先意味着什么。事实上,"它是什么"和"谁来定义它"是新公共服务倡导者仍在争论的热点问题。

第七章

全球化与网络治理的兴起

世界在变化,而且变化很快!随着公共管理在全球化时代的不断发展,当代各国政府在国内必须面对的许多问题都来自境外的国家和地区。地方公共管理者在直接解决这些源于国外的问题时会受其能力限制,他们必须适应在越来越不稳定,因此也越来越不可预测的环境中工作。事实上,通常与相对稳定的以国家为中心的体系相关联的"理性化"过程,正在被一个以"非理性"和"混乱"为特征的没有人负责的新时代所超越。

许多与公共治理和管理有关的行政活动传统上由国家控制,现在则由政府和非政府组织(NGOs)、私营公司、独立机构和公民团体组成的松散网络控制。这种国际网络通常围绕着一套特定的相关政策或行政议题或关注点而组织起来,可能包括了同时在地方、区域、国家和国际层面运作的个人与团体。在通常被称为"网络治理"或"通过网络治理"的情况下,多个国内和国际行动主体的参与可能会阻碍主权治理机构成功实施公共政策的努力。当代公共管理者被迫在如此多样的环境下运作,不得不发展新的建立共识的技能,以便将不同的国内和国际团体聚集在一起,追求集体目标。让我们更深入地看看这些网络方法。

正如我们所讨论的,全球化的力量迫使公共管理者越来越多地将注意力转向跨国形式的治理。在这方面,传统的自上而下的组织系统已不适合解决需要国际合作的复杂的全球问题和危机。在过去的几十年里,通过多层政府运作的组织松散的公共和私营机构网络,在公共管理中发挥着越来越大的作用。

在网络治理型系统中,权力和权威往往分散在各种自主的利益相关者之间,其运作超出了国家政府的范围和控制。从全球气候变化到人类安全,治理网络围绕价值观、关注点、议题和问题进行组织,其规模和范围可能会有很大差异。它们的组织结构灵活多变,允许参与者随着环境的变化进出网络。例如,为了应对来自国外的特定恐怖威胁,美国国土安全部(DHS)必须与联邦调查局(FBI)、中央情报局(CIA)、国家安全局(NSA)和地方警察机构等国内组织以及国际刑警组织(INTERPOL)等国际情报机构进行沟通和协调。随着周围威胁环境的变化,可能还会与其他机构和团体建立新的伙伴关系。现在让我们看一些例子,说明市、地区和国家各级组织的治理网络在应对气候变化危机方面是如何发挥作用的(方框11)。

方框11 政策和行政网络的类型

1. 信息:成员们分享想法和知识,他们用这些想法和知识来指导他们自己在本组织中的工作。
2. 发展型:成员交换信息和想法。提供教育资源以帮助员工发展提高绩效的能力。
3. 外联：除了帮助成员参与信息和发展活动，网络成员还分享客户联系信息和资源机会。
4. 行动：成员们努力改变他们所在组织的政策和常规，以帮助实现网络的共同目标。正式的合作包括共享资金、提供服务或为网络的未来使用开发共同的资源。

资料来源：罗伯特·阿格拉诺夫，《网络管理：为公共组织增值》，第10页

　　今天，世界上七十亿人口中的大多数生活在城市和其他大都市区。毫不奇怪，世界上最大的城市产生了世界上大部分的垃圾和污染。更具体地说，大都市区现在总共产生了世界三分之二以上的二氧化碳排放，这是全球气候变化的主要原因。受庞大的官僚机构和烦琐的政治程序的拖累，各国政府在实质性的政策变革和行政行动方面反应迟缓。与最近的全球化趋势相关联的国家实力的削弱，使得世界各地的市政和区域机构有勇气在减少其二氧化碳排放总量方面发挥主导作用。一些地方领导人和代表世界上最大城市的管理者，一直在通过被称为"跨国城市网络"（TMNs）的组织来进行合作，以实现这一目标。由与国际组织和私营公司结成伙伴关系的地方政府、世界大都市协会等政治上强大的"跨国城市网络"以及联合国环境与发展会议（UNCED）等国际发展组织组成，在动员跨国努力应对主要城市地区面临的气候变化和相关挑战方面非常成功。1992年，环发会议最初只有三座城市，在不到二十年的时间里，成员增加到一百多个。伦敦市市长肯·利文斯通渴望自己的城市在这

个紧迫的问题上起带头作用,他成立了一个由主要城市组成的财团,后来被称为C40。如今,C40是管理气候变化问题最有影响力的市级网络之一,它采用各种市场和规划工具来规避传统上僵化和正规的以国家为中心的官僚机构。C40已经发展到近七十个不同规模和范围的城市,并于2011年与世界银行成功合作,建立了"测量温室气体排放的共同标准"。当这些标准被世界银行的气候投资基金采用,以帮助他们更好地了解资金和投资决策时,C40宣告了胜利。

城市领导人并不是唯一利用国际网络来应对全球气候变化的人。例如,美国的州和地区领导人已经启动了他们自己的治理网络。亚利桑那州州长珍妮特·纳波利塔诺决心采取及时和实质性的政策措施来降低美国西部地区的二氧化碳排放,她大胆地宣布:"在缺乏有意义的联邦行动的情况下,应该由各州采取行动来应对气候变化并减少该国的温室气体排放。"震惊于西部各州"正受到气候变化影响的重创",这位亚利桑那州的领导人与来自加利福尼亚州、俄勒冈州、新墨西哥州和华盛顿州的其他五位州长一起,对温室气体排放实施了严格的地区限制。为了确保工业化程度更高的州得到相称的对待,这个大胆的组织采用了一种区域性的"总量管制和交易"计划,允许成员州购买和出售被保持在这些区域限制内的二氧化碳排放额度。2009年,加利福尼亚州州长阿诺德·施瓦辛格与联合国开发计划署(UNDP)和联合国环境规划署(UNEP)合作主办了一次全球气候变化峰会,以制定合作倡议,促进可持续能源的生产和使用。来自世界各地七十多个州和省的三十多位州长、地方官员、商界领袖和政策专家出席了会议,令人印象深刻。

国际网络也正在成为发展中国家跨国水治理的重要参与者。重要水源的过度开采和过度污染已经在亚洲、非洲和拉丁美洲的部分地区造成了公共卫生和可持续性危机。联合国在2003年发布的首份《水资源开发报告》中，宣布"水危机本质上是一场治理危机，在如何更有效地治理水资源方面，社会正面临许多社会、经济和政治挑战"。与此相关，可持续发展问题世界首脑会议强调了发展公私部门合作伙伴关系，以履行与至关重要的水资源的调节、维护和分配相关的行政职能。

过去的二十年来，印度国家政府采取了大胆的私有化举措，以改善全国的水资源管理。作为这项工作的一部分，该国的联邦政府和邦政府一直与国际金融机构（如世界银行和亚洲开发银行）、私营企业和非政府组织合作。为了使该国陈旧的水利基础设施现代化，中央城市发展部做出了巨大努力，消除了对新资本项目外国直接投资的保护主义壁垒，取消了对外国来源的饮用水设施和设备的进口限制。与此相关的是，印度工业联合会（CII）和印度水事商业联盟（IBAW）一直在与国际机构合作，例如联合国开发计划署和美国国际开发署（USAID），并扩大商业部门的参与和介入。印度的中央政府还同时与在日内瓦、斯德哥尔摩和华盛顿特区工作的国际专家顾问合作，提供与饮用水监测和分配有关的急需技术和管理专业知识。

让我们在结束关于网络治理的讨论时，先简要考察一下信息技术是如何塑造新的行政流程模式的。世界各地的政府一直在采用新的信息和通信技术（ICTs）来提高符合新公共管理原则的行政效率，并根据新公共服务强调的民主价值观加强公民与政府的关系。众所周知的"电子政务"现象正在重塑我们所知的公共管理。"电子政务"一词的一般用法，是指与公共部门治理有关的信息技术的各种用途。与此相关，管理专家格兰特和周认为，电子政务的核心目的是：（1）发展和提供高质量、无缝和综合的公共服务；（2）实现有效的组织成员关系管理；（3）支持地方、州、国家和国际各层级公民、企业和民间社会的经济和社会发展目标。

由于认识到其工业竞争力有赖于创造持续和无限制地访问公共维护的信息源，瑞典政府于2000年通过了一项历史性的法律，承诺"一个人人共享的信息社会"。瑞典公共管理署为了消除组织之间的行政分歧，通过了一项全面的信息和通信技术方案，将传统的层级公共机构转变为所谓的"电子网络"开放机构。今天，整个工业化世界的国家和地方政府都效仿瑞典，大力投资于电子政务基础设施，以促进公开获取公共信息，从而改善民主监督和问责制。因此，公民实际上可以不受限制地访问公共记录和政府官方文件，如财产税记录、历史地图、公共听证会记录和公务员工资。

然而，对于各级政府的管理者来说，管理和保护包含在许多公共文档中的公民个人数据已被证明是一项艰巨的挑战。整合不同来源的公共信息并使其广泛可用，会对个人隐私造成严重威胁。许多国家对此的反应是，通过严格的法律来管控公共管理者处理、传输、共享、存储和访问某些类型敏感信息的方式。与此同时，如前所述，在许多具体情况下，公职人员和公民都必须能够访问公共部门组织管理的庞大信息系统和数据库。因此，这些系统特别容易受到互联网黑客和犯罪网络发起的攻击。事实上，现在花费了大量纳税人的钱和无数的人力时间在安全系统和员工数据管理培训上，以减少这些威胁。对公共机构数据系统的犯罪攻击，每年给国家及其地方政府造成数亿美元的损失。

网络治理以各种形式和伪装在公共管理中发挥着重要作用。威斯特伐利亚建立的"现代国家"的概念及其提供公共服务的传统手段和方法正在被重新定义。新形式的公私"协作"关系已经取代了它的位置。新一代反思型公共管理者如果要在不断变化的全球环境下领导他们的组织，就必须具备新的技能。正如我们所见，在民主社会中，网络治理可以发挥许多重要的功能。例如，创新通常是通过政府官方办公室之外运作的机构和个人的参与所带来的补充知识和专业知识来促进的。此外，由于网络的流动性和灵活的组织结构，网络可以在紧迫问题出现时立即适应和迅速应对。然而，与此同时，鉴于网络的高度复杂性和分散的结构，组织的目标和目的可能变得模糊和复杂。此外，当行政程序转移到私营部门或半公共机构时，政府正式提供的公共产品和服务的官方监督就不再能够得到保证。由于政府不再掌握政策和行政程序，公众问责和责任也很容易被牺牲掉。

第八章

公共管理的未来

正如我们所看到的,公共管理的专业研究和实践都异常活跃。因此,它们的未来是无法预测的。虽然从废物管理到公共教育等基本公共服务不会很快消失,但其行政职能的实施和评估方式却有可能变化很大。正如我们在短暂的旅程中所看到的,全球层面发生的巨大变化正在给公共管理带来根本性的转变。由于无法保护国内政治、经济和社会事务免受全球化的强大影响,公共管理者被迫在高度不稳定和多变的环境中履行其职能和任务。为了吸引新的全球金融投资,现代政府一直在进行一场激烈的"逐底竞赛",以大幅削减公共预算。在一个以"不确定性"日益增加为特征的全球化世界中,各级政府的公共管理者被迫实施紧缩预算的政策。他们必须以完全不同的方式思考21世纪的治理意味着什么。

2008年全球金融危机爆发后,普华永道会计师事务所建立的公共部门研究中心(PSRC)发表了一份题为《提供公共服务的未来之路》的报告。这份报告概述了政府机构为了长期成功而必须发展的特定核心能力。除了强调"公私合作、共同投资、共同创造和共同设计作为'必须具备的'能力",该报告还强调,公共组织应该变得越来越"敏捷、互联和透明"。它呼吁公共部门领导人在这一进程中成为重要的"变革推动者"。它强调以系统为导向的领导力,而不是传统的以任务为中心的管理,敦促公共部门领导人为其机构给出一个清晰的新愿景。根据新公共服务提出的目标,公共部门研究中心的报告强调面向公民的服务是公共部门的最高优先事项。因此,政府工作的重点首先应该是"激励"内部和外部的利益相关者。它们应鼓励公共管理者与他们所服务的公民合作,以便发现公民的问题并设计创新的解决办法。

今天的公共管理者面临着满足公民日益增长的高要求的挑战。英国市场调查公司(Ipsos MORI)对十个国家的五千名公民进行了"公共服务满意度"调查。它揭示了41%的美国公民对政府管理公共服务的方式"不满意"。有趣的是,这与澳大利亚、巴西、加拿大、法国、德国、印度、意大利、新加坡和英国等国家明显不同,这些国家受访者的"满意"水平平均接近65%。当被问及他们认为政府最重要的关注点应该是什么时,大多数美国受访者表示,他们希望政府"以更具成本收益的方式提供服务"。奇怪的是,虽然五十岁至六十四岁的美国公民对政府提供的服务的成本和质量"最不满意",但三十五岁以下的人却乐观地认为,美国政府将能够满足他们"未来五年的需求和期望"。调查进一步显示,一般来说,公民希望在当今"高度接触"的社会中看到公共服务管理方式的重大改进。除了要求更个性化的服务,公民对公共部门治理中增加"透明度"

和"问责制"的要求也越来越苛刻。

下一个十年

正如我们在第七章中看到的,通过新形式的电子政务,普通公民可以一天二十四小时获得越来越多的政府服务和信息。事实上,基于互联网的服务的激增为各种公共机构提供了与公民直接互动的新方法。然而,与此同时,增加参与政策和行政程序的机会可能是一把双刃剑。随着准入的增加,对政策和行政程序的审查也在增加。例如,批评者指责说,一旦政治大门向心怀不满的个人敞开,情绪化的民意将取代冷静的政策讨论和理性的辩论。

在创造"更精简、更吝啬"的政府形式的幌子下,美国等国家的中间偏右政治运动一直在对公共部门发起政治攻击。然而,正如我们所看到的,在一些国家,由公务员部门的角色变化产生的问题往往比其他国家更少对抗性,或至少更少党派性。尽管对"大政府"进行了无情的言辞攻击,但公共部门的作用并没有明显减弱。事实上,最近的数据证实,公共部门支出继续稳步增长。例如在美国,公共支出目前占国内生产总值的42%,而1960年时仅为28%。虽然在全球金融危机后的几年里,2009年至2014年间略有下降,但总体趋势表明,公共部门支出将继续增长。同样值得注意的是,政府收入(占该国国内生产总值的比例)已经下降。这反过来给公共机构和在其中服务的管理者带来了前所未有的压力。随着与移民、全球气候变化、外来疾病暴发等相关的挑战在未来变得越来越复杂,公共管理者的负担只会增加。(公共支出增长的历史概况见图3)

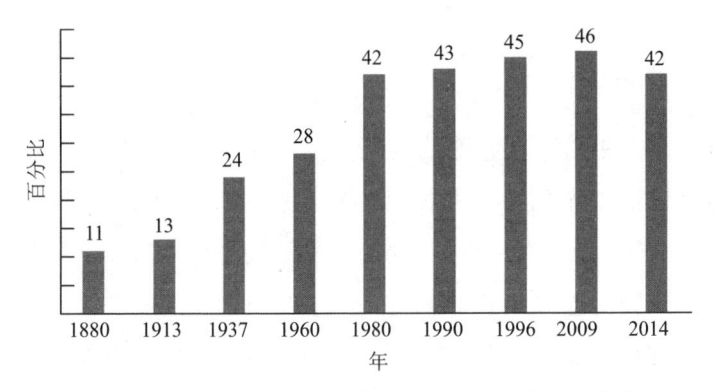

图 3　1880年至2014年高收入国家和经合组织国家政府支出占国内生产总值的百分比

世界人口现已超过七十亿，并且还在继续增长。一些研究预测，它将在十年内达到八十亿。预期寿命的提高、家庭结构的变化和失业率的上升，迫使美国决策者推出一系列新的公共服务和额外的福利支持。随着所谓的婴儿潮一代临近退休，公共养老金和医疗保健系统将面临前所未有的压力。目前，六十五岁以上的美国公民占比近15%。预计这一数字将在十年内增加到18%以上。这意味着近五分之一的公民将有资格享受公共退休福利。目前，美国90%以上的老年人接受医疗保险福利，目前每年花费美国纳税人超过五千亿美元。根据公共部门研究中心的报告，到2015年，为该国日益增长的老年人口提供公共服务所需的联邦、州和地方费用估计将高达每年九千四百亿美元（占国内生产总值的4.4%）。

最近的2015年欧洲金融危机暴露了希腊、西班牙和葡萄牙等欧洲南部经济体长期存在的深层结构性弱点。除了必须应对与青年长期失业相关的挑战，这些国家的政府还被迫为越来越多的退休人员扩大公共服务。事实上，在全世界先进的工业化国家中,老年公民人口的占比正在急剧增加。

不幸的是,政策制定者和公共管理者之间关于如何最好地在危机发生前避免危机(并在危机发生后解决危机)的大部分战略讨论和辩论,往往是在相互排斥的意识形态术语中进行的,如"政府与市场"。这些错误的二分法无法为决策者和管理者提供识别问题的有用视角,结果就会经常阻止他们设计务实的解决方案。公共官员和管理者应着重发展足够的政府主导的监管机构和政策,以支持市场良好地运转。

任何一个国家公共部门的健康和活力都与其私营经济的状况密切相关。回顾自大萧条(20世纪30年代)以来最严重的衰退,2008年毁灭性的全球金融崩溃将会留下尚不清楚的长期影响。从长期来看,美国目前从未来借款来支付公共项目和服务的做法是不可持续的。与此同时,像许多欧洲国家一样,削减基本公共服务和项目可能会带来可怕的后果。通过养老金、公共医疗服务、公共教育和社会保险提供的社会安全网,只能在不影响整个欧洲民主政府合法性的情况下收缩。

毫无疑问,单一民族国家及其公共管理系统未来将会面临一系列新的挑战。一些人认为,这些挑战将公务员置于难以维系的境地。然而,其他人声称,这些新的挑战正在为公共管理者创造历史性的机会,以促成有意义的积极变革。在过去,行政改革是根据每个国家独特的社会结构、制度配置和历史传统而形成的。然而,近年来,我们目睹了快速的全球经济和社会的变化,这些变化正在挑战传统的行政规范和做法。因此,公共管理和领导力最重要的焦点应该是雇用拥有"正确"技能组合的"正确"个人,以应对我们的文明在全球化时代面临的巨大挑战。

索 引

（条目后的数字为原书页码，见本书边码）

A

Affordable Care Act (ACA) (Obamacare) 《平价医疗法案》(奥巴马医改) 6—7
Australia 澳大利亚 4
　New Public Management (NPM) 新公共管理 63, 65, 71—74
　urban density 城市密度 14

B

Basic Law (Germany)《基本法》(德国) 49
Beveridge Report《贝弗里奇报告》57—59
Bismarck, Otto Von 奥托·冯·俾斯麦 38
Blair, Tony 托尼·布莱尔 75, 78—79
Bonnin, Charles-Jean 夏尔-让·博朗 37—38
Britain 英国，见 United Kingdom
Bureaucracy 官僚机构 40—42
business, running of governments as 政府像企业一样运营 7—10

C

C40 (Cities Climate Leadership Group) C40（城市气候领导联盟）96

Cameron, David 戴维·卡梅伦 8
Capitalism 资本主义 47—48, 61
China, urban density 中国的城市密度 13
civil leadership 公民领导力 2
climate change 气候变化 96—97
Clinton, Bill 比尔·克林顿 74—77
communication between organizations 组织之间的交流 85—88
Comprehensive Spending Reviews (CSRs) 全面支出审查 78

D

decentralization 权力下放 25—26
Deming, W. Edwards W. 爱德华兹·戴明 84—87
democracy 民主 15, 17—18, 28—29, 58
　'bottom-up'"自下而上" 23
　Democracy Index 民主指数 92
　Western 西方 47—49
Denhardt, Robert B. and Janet V. Denhardt 罗伯特·B. 登哈特和珍妮特·V. 登哈特 89—90
deregulation 解除管制 75—76

E

East India Company 东印度公司 27
economics, global 世界经济 45—47, 101—102
e-governance 电子政务 98—99
electoral processes 选举过程 28—29
emergency responses 紧急响应 11—13

employment 就业 35, 42, 46, 60
 China 中国 13
 civil service 公务员 29—30
 Sweden 瑞典 44
 USA 美国 55, 77
 Works Progress Administration (WPA) 公共事业振兴署 53
employment schemes 就业计划 53, 77, 79
English Civil War 英国内战（1642—1649）18
Europe 欧洲
 financial crisis (2015) 金融危机（2015）105
 progressive reform 渐进式改革 35—36

F

Fayol, Henri 亨利·法约尔 38
Financial Management Improvement Programme《财政管理改进方案》（FMIP）72—74
France 法国 36

G

Germany 德国 38—42
 welfare policy 福利政策 48—50
Gladstone, William 威廉·格莱斯顿 34
global financial crises 1930s 20世纪30年代全球金融危机 45—46
 2008 2008年全球金融危机 101—102

globalization 全球化 10—14, 93—100
global population 全球人口 104
golden age of managed capitalism 管理资本主义的黄金时代 47—48
Government Business Enterprises (GBEs) 政府商业企业 72—74
Great Depression 大萧条 45—46
Gulick, Luther 卢瑟·古利克 54—55

H

Hamilton, Alexander 亚历山大·汉密尔顿 22
Harvey, J. T. 哈维 8
Hawke, Robert 罗伯特·霍克 72
healthcare 医疗保健 55—56, 66, 71
Hobbes, Thomas 托马斯·霍布斯 18
Hurricane Katrina 卡特里娜飓风 11—13

I

India 印度
 networks 网络 97—98
 urban density 城市密度 13
industrialization 工业化 42—43
 global 全球 10—14
information and communication technologies (ICTs) 信息和通信技术 98—100
interdependence between organizations 组织之间的相互依赖 85—88
international networks 国际网络 93—96

J

Jackson, Andrew 安德鲁·杰克逊 28
Jefferson, Thomas 托马斯·杰斐逊 22—24

K

Keating, Michael 迈克尔·基廷 63
Keating, Paul 保罗·基廷 72
Kettl, Donald 唐纳德·凯特尔 20, 63
Keynes, John Maynard 约翰·梅纳德·凯恩斯 46—47

L

Leadership 领导力 2, 84
learning organizations 学习型组织 81—84, 88
Lewis, H. S. 刘易斯 2
Locke, John 约翰·洛克 19—20

M

macroeconomics 宏观经济学 46
Madison, James 詹姆斯·麦迪逊 20—22
management 管理 89—92
mass production 大规模生产
Medium Term Financial Strategy (MTFS) 中期财政战略 68

N

Napoleonic tradition 拿破仑传统 36—37
national insurance 国民保险 35, 51
nation-states 民族国家 35—36, 44
neoliberalism 新自由主义 64—65, 74, 76—77
networks 网络 93—100
New Economics 新经济学 84
New Federalism 新联邦制 65—67
New Public Administration (NPA) 新公共行政 62—63
New Public Management (NPM) 新公共管理 63—80
New Public Service (NPS) 新公共服务 89—92
Niskanen, William A. 威廉·A. 尼斯卡宁 66—67

O

Obama, President Barack 巴拉克·奥巴马总统 6—7, 9—10
Obamacare (Affordable Care Act) 奥巴马医改(《平价医疗法案》) 6—7
organizational systems 组织系统 84—88, 94

P

Peace of Westphalia《威斯特伐利亚和约》17
Pendleton Act (1883)《彭德尔顿法

案》30
political science 政治学 30—31
Poor Law (1834)《济贫法》32—34
popular sovereignty 人民主权 17—19
population 人口 13—14
POSDCORB 管理的七个基本功能 54—55
poverty 贫困 54—55, 57—58
private sector 私营部门 7—9, 62, 64, 66
privatization 私有化 69—70
public opinion of governments 政府的民意 4—5, 102—103
public sector 公共部门 103—105

R

Railtrack 铁路轨道公司 9
Reagan, President Ronald 罗纳德·里根总统 65—67
Reflective practice 反思实践 81—84
Reich, Robert B. 罗伯特·B. 赖克 48
Roosevelt, President Franklin D. (FDR) 富兰克林·D. 罗斯福总统 52—54

S

Scandinavia 斯堪的纳维亚 42—44
Second World War 第二次世界大战 55
Simon, Herbert 赫伯特·西蒙 56
Social Democratic governments (Sweden) 社会民主党政府(瑞典) 50—52

social market economy 社会市场经济 49
social policy reform 社会政策改革 79
social reform 社会改革 29, 43—44
Social Security Act (USA)《社会保障法案》(美国) 54
Stein, Lorenz Von 洛伦兹·冯·施泰因 39
stock market crash (USA, 1929) 股票市场崩溃(美国,1929年) 52
strategic planning cycles 战略规划周期 91
Sweden 瑞典 42—44
    information and communication 信息和通信 99
    welfare policy 福利政策 50—52

T

Tammany Hall 坦慕尼协会 29
taxes 税收 51, 67—68
Taylor, Frederick Winslow 弗雷德里克·温斯洛·泰勒 31—32
terrorist attacks 恐怖袭击 4—5
Thatcher, Margaret 玛格丽特·撒切尔 8, 60, 63, 67—71, 79
transnational municipal networks (TMNs) 跨国城市网络 96
Trevelyan-Northcote Report (1854)《杜维廉-诺思科特报告》34

U

United Kingdom 英国 3

decentralization 权力下放 25
healthcare 医疗保健 71
New Public Management (NPM) 新公共管理 63—64, 67—71, 75, 78—79
popular sovereignty 人民主权 18—19
privatization 私有化 9, 69—70
welfare policy 福利政策 32—35, 57—60, 79

United Nations (UN) 联合国 Conference on Environment and Development (UNCED) 环境与发展会议 96

environmental initiatives 环境倡议 97

United States of America (USA) 美利坚合众国(美国) 3, 4
  Affordable Care Act (ACA)《平价医疗法案》6—7
  decentralization 权力下放 25—26
  government shutdown 政府关闭 5—7
  healthcare 医疗保健 55—36, 66
  Hurricane Katrina 卡特里娜飓风 11—13
  independence and formation of government 独立和政府的形成 19—24
  networks 网络 96—97
  New Public Management (NPM) 新公共管理 65—67, 74—77
  population 人口 104—105
  progressive reforms 渐进式改革 28—32
  public sector 公共部门 103
  Tea Party 茶党 9—10

urban density 城市密度 14
welfare policy 福利政策 52—57, 77
urban density 城市密度 13—14
Urwick, Lyndall 林德尔·厄威克 54—55

W

Waldo, Dwight 德怀特·瓦尔多 56, 62
water facilities 供水设施 97—98
Weber, Max 马克斯·韦伯 39—42
welfare states 福利国家 32—35, 47—60, 77, 79
Westphalian Treaty《威斯特伐利亚和约》17
Wilson, President Woodrow 伍德罗·威尔逊总统 30—31
Works Progress Administration (WPA) 公共事业振兴署 53

Stella Z. Theodoulou and Ravi K. Roy

PUBLIC ADMINISTRATION

A Very Short Introduction

Contents

Preface xiii

List of abbreviations xvii

List of illustrations xix

List of tables xxi

1 A contemporary overview 1

2 The journey from Westphalia to Philadelphia 17

3 Progressive reform across the globe 27

4 The rise of the modern welfare state 45

5 The New Public Management goes global 61

6 The new administrative age 81

7 Globalization and the rise of network governance 93

8 The future of public administration 101

References and further reading 107

Preface

What does it mean to be an effective public administrator in the modern global age? In the further pages of our brief introduction, we invite you to join us on a whirlwind journey of the field and professional practice of public administration. Along the way, we will explore how the field and practice has evolved over time from its beginnings to the current era. In the course of our historical survey, we will unpack some of the essential leadership and management principles that have characteristically defined what it means to be an effective public administrator.

What is public administration and why is it important? In order to accomplish collective goals of society, civic leaders must learn how to organize and manage public bureaucracies. More specifically, one might say that public administration is the 'art' of management and leadership involved in developing and delivering essential public services required to sustain modern civilization. Covering areas from public safety and social welfare to transportation and education, the services provided through the public sector remain an inextricable part of our daily lives. Consider, for example, what life would be like in the absence of public services and utilities such as public roads and highways, emergency medical services, information network infrastructure, and water and power. Often times, we tend to take these essential 'public goods' for granted. Most of us simply go about our day with little thought or understanding about the complex processes involved in providing them. Worse still, it has become fashionable to blame all of the problems plaguing modern society on 'big government' and 'lazy fat cat public bureaucrats'.

Such uncharitable characterizations have been reinforced in the recent political campaigns currently being waged among those belonging to America's political right. The truth is, however, mounting political pressure is being exerted by those belonging to both the political right and left of the ideological spectrum to slash many of these essential services to the bone. Stemming from demands for greater economic austerity, modern governments all across the globe are being forced to 'do much more with much less'. This trend is expected to continue well into the foreseeable future and hence will be considered the 'new normal' for public administrators operating in today's world. Forced to work in increasingly fierce political climates where government is seen as 'the problem and not the solution', public administrators have been compelled to radically re-think how they govern in the modern age.

Public sector agencies face unprecedented challenges as droves of baby boomers retire from within their ranks, thereby opening the door to a new generation of qualified, well-trained leaders and managers to assume these indispensable government posts. Aspiring public managers and leaders must develop an understanding of the role of the public sector and how it is being reshaped in the global age if they are to be worthy candidates for these employment opportunities. The recent explosion in the number of applicants seeking admission to both graduate and undergraduate programmes in public administration across the globe attests to this.

While we recognize that there is no shortage of textbooks and other literary sources that may provide solid and comprehensive treatments on the theories related to the field, few have synthesized these elements into a crisp and highly readable narrative. We invite the reader on a compelling journey that surveys some of the major historical movements and trends that informed the origins and continued evolution of this fascinating topic. Indeed, we take the reader through an exploration of the concrete manifestations of these trends in various countries and regions around the world. Providing much more than a simple overview, along the way, we will tackle some of the most hotly debated issues of our time, including: whether 'government should be run like a business' or whether the privatization of public services is always the appropriate means for producing improved quality and lowering costs for taxpayers; and whether governments' surveillance efforts to protect their citizens against terrorism are encroaching on personal privacy and individual liberty.

Drawing on our experiences and intellectual expertise, we have carefully crafted our discussion in a manner that will resonate well with audiences in the US, Canada, the UK, Europe, and Australia. Additionally, many of the case studies used to illustrate the themes discussed in this volume were specifically tailored to our readers in Asia and Latin America. In order to better prepare contemporary public managers to meet the monumental challenges that await them, this narrative focuses on the essential history and contextual background of the field. Dealing with a highly complex topic by nature, this volume will provide practical insights that will help public administrators ask better questions when approaching contemporary dilemmas.

In keeping with the accessible tone of this *Very Short Introduction* series we have kept our discussion here rather selective and general. Pitched at a level that will be appealing to the lay interested reader, our aim is to present our readers with an engaging overview of this very rich and highly complex subject. Readers who have successfully acquired a basic understanding of the topics and themes discussed in our brief volume will likely be prepared to delve more deeply into the subject matter. For those readers, we invite them to consult the concluding reference section for a list of books and other sources offering more detailed and nuanced discussions and analysis.

We would like to thank our colleagues and friends at California State University Northridge, Southern Utah University, Claremont Graduate University, and the University of California, Santa Barbara for providing us with valuable support. We would like to extend special appreciation to Andrea Keegan and her wonderful team at Oxford University Press. We would also like to express our deepest love and gratitude to our respective families. Joan, Nicole, Yianna, Marti, and Alex, se agapáme! Indeed countless people have been consulted in preparing this book to whom we are deeply indebted; its remaining shortcomings remain our sole responsibility.

List of abbreviations

ACA	Affordable Care Act
AfD	Germany's Alternative for Germany
ALPG	Australian Labour Party Governments
APS	Australian Public Service
AT&T	American Telephone and Telegraph
C40	C40 Cities Climate Leadership Group
CIA	Central Intelligence Agency
CII	Confederation of Indian Industry
CNN	Cable News Network
DCFS	Department of Family and Children Services
DLC	Democratic Leadership Council
EPA	Environmental Protection Agency
EU	European Union
FBI	Federal Bureau of Investigation
FDI	Foreign Direct Investment
FDR	Franklin D. Roosevelt
FEMA	Federal Emergency Management Agency
FMIP	Financial Management Improvement Programme
GATT	General Agreement on Tariffs and Trade
GBE	Government Business Enterprises
GDP	Gross Domestic Product
GRH	Gramm-Rudman-Hollings Initiative
IBAW	Indian Business Alliance on Water
ICTs	information and communication technologies
IMF	International Monetary Fund
INTERPOL	International Criminal Policy Agency
LNPCG	Liberal-National Party Coalition Government
MPA	Master of Public Administration

MTFS	Medium Term Financial Strategy
NAFTA	North American Free Trade Agreement
NGOs	non-governmental organizations
NHS	National Health Service (UK)
NPA	New Public Administration
NPM	New Public Management
NPS	New Public Service
NSA	National Security Agency
OECD	Organisation for Economic Co-operation and Development
OPEC	Organization of Petroleum Exporting Countries
PSRC	Public Sector Research Centre
SAP	Swedish Social Democratic Labour Party
SoPK	System of Profound Knowledge
TQM	total quality management
UKIP	UK Independence Party
UNCED	United Nations Conference on Environment and Development
UNDP	United Nations Development Programme
UNEP	United Nations Environment Programme
USAID	United States Agency for International Development

List of illustrations

1. New Orleans underwater **11**
   © FEMA / Alamy Stock Photo.

2. Urban density challenges **14**
   © TonyV3112 / Shutterstock.com.

3. Government expenditure as a percentage of GDP, 1880–2014 **104**
   Data taken from Tanzi: Ludger Schuknecht, *Public Spending in the 20th Century: A Global Perspective* (Cambridge University Press, 2008); and Vito Tanzi, *The Economic Role of the State in the 21st Century*. Originally published in *Cato Journal*, 25(3) (Fall 2005), pp. 619 © The Cato Institute. Used by permission. OECD, 'Social expenditure update: Social spending is falling in some countries, but in many others it remains at historically high levels', p. 1. <www.oecd.org/social/expenditure.htm>. 2014 Index of Economic Freedom 'Explore the Data' (The Heritage Foundation, 2014).

List of tables

1. Year of introduction of various social services in selected nations **47**

2. Government employment, 1870–1980 **60**
   OECD (2015), 'Employment in the public sector', *Government at a Glance 2000–2015*, OECD Publishing, Paris. DOI: http://dx.doi.org/10.1787/gov_glance-2015-22-en; adapted from Messaoud Hammouya, 'Statistics on public sector employment: methodology, structures and trends' (Bureau of Statistics International Labour Office, Geneva, 1999) © ILO, 1999.

3. Characteristics of a learning organization **82**
   Gipsie Ranney, slide presentation on 'Deming's Ideas in the Twenty-first Century', The In2In Network Forum Meetings at California State University Northridge on 20 June 2014.

Chapter 1
A contemporary overview

During a recent college recruitment fair that we attended, a prospective student approached one of our faculty representatives and sharply asked, 'What is public administration and what kind of job can I get with a degree in your field?' The career-minded young woman went on to proclaim, 'I mean, I have heard of the field, of course—everyone has. But what exactly is it and what do you teach?' She had raised a serious question and, perhaps without even realizing it, stumbled onto an ongoing debate that has long been raging among academics and practitioners alike. Pressed to provide an immediate explanation, the faculty member simply said that 'public administration involves the countless activities that are performed by officials in the delivery of essential public services to our nation's citizens. Public administrators', the faculty member went on to explain, 'serve in roles ranging from law enforcement to civic planning, and they may be working in agencies from the local town hall all the way to the White House. In the simplest terms, as instructors, we aim to provide our students in public administration with the professional leadership and management skills required for them to properly "administer" these essential services.' While this brief explanation seemed to satisfy the questioner with a useful glimpse into the field, there is certainly much more to the story. We, therefore, invite you to join us as we explore this complex and fascinating topic in greater depth.

Although the concept of the 'career civil administrator' is often historically identified with the Mesopotamian Empire almost 4,000 years ago, primordial forms of tribal leadership can be traced back 10,000 years BC to the Stone Age. Indeed as cultural anthropologist Herbert S. Lewis noted, 'leadership is a basic element in the organization of group activity in society...leadership lies at or near the heart of most political life, political competition and strife'. Human beings have always looked to civil leaders to oversee the various activities required to sustain groups of people who live together. To be sure, the role of civil leadership varies widely among cultures in accordance with the responsibilities that they are expected to perform and the powers that they wield. Whether in the form of tribal chiefs, magisterial monarchs, or democratically elected officials, civil leaders will be needed in any society to make decisions and mobilize the resources required to achieve its goals. Civil leaders, however, depend on a wide array of subordinate 'officials' to carry out these goals. The countless 'official' activities involved in carrying out these goals may be collectively referred to as the 'art' of public administration.

At its core, public administration refers to the wide array of leadership and management functions and mandates that are carried out by civil officials involved with public sector 'governance'. According to Laurence E. Lynn, Jr, Carolyn J. Heinrich, and Carolyn J. Hill, governance involves 'regimes, laws, rules, judicial decisions, and administrative practices that constrain, prescribe, and enable the provisions of publicly supported goals and services'. Touching every aspect of our daily lives, public administration includes the continuous processes, routines, actions, behaviours, and discretionary decisions that rank and file bureaucrats operating at the 'street level' exercise on a day-to-day basis. Public administration, therefore, involves much more than the authoritative actions undertaken by higher level public officials. Indeed millions of public administrators serve in areas related to civic planning, public transportation, budgeting, policy evaluation, election monitoring and oversight, law enforcement and fire, as well as social services ranging from healthcare to unemployment assistance and job retraining. As indicated by the faculty member to the prospective student attending the college fair, public administrators serve in positions ranging from the president or prime minister of a country and the members of their cabinets all the way down to local municipal parking enforcement officers.

The interaction among public authorities and agencies involved in the governing process is highly complex. America's relatively fragmented administrative system, for example, is comprised of a national government that shares governing responsibility and authority with fifty state governments and nearly 90,000 other units operating at the county, municipal, and district levels. Staffed with millions of public administrators, America's enormous public sector provides essential services to its citizens, ranging from public works and child protection to food safety and rehabilitation. Britain, by contrast, has possessed a relatively centralized system in which the national government delegates specific functions and mandates to various 'subnational' administrative divisions. Local administration in Britain is dispersed over 300 districts, which themselves are divided into metropolitan and non-metropolitan districts. These districts are overseen by mayors and district councils. Covering areas from public transport and housing all the way to public health and education, these agencies provide vital services. By its very nature, governance is intertwined with politics. Let us look at this in further detail.

The great political paradox

Over time the functions and mandates of public administrators have grown exponentially in response to citizen demands. The expectations placed on government to provide and manage ever-increasing amounts of publicly funded student loans and government resources to support small private businesses are quintessential examples. The great paradox is that as citizens' demands and expectations for public sector services continue to grow, public satisfaction with 'government' seems simultaneously to decline. One well-known scholar even suggested that US citizens want to severely limit government from interfering in their private lives via higher taxes and security-related surveillance, while simultaneously insisting on increased government support to assist them when they deem it necessary. Indeed, public opinion polls in the US consistently confirm that most citizens hold negative views towards government, characteristically associating public bureaucracies with 'waste' and 'inefficiency'. America is not alone. In a CNN editorial on 11 June 2013, the Director of Global Economic Attitudes for the renowned Pew Research Center revealed that while nearly 75 per cent of Australian residents were satisfied with their personal economic circumstances, less than 50 per cent were satisfied with the direction of government. Dissatisfaction with 'government' and 'public bureaucrats' is a sentiment that is increasingly being echoed across many European countries as well.

Buzzwords like 'accountability', 'efficiency', and 'performance' have become the political rallying cries of the popular 'good governance' crusade that has been gaining traction across the globe. In recent times, right-of-centre political movements have echoed these themes to promote fiscal austerity and secure deep cuts in government resources. To some extent, these sentiments reflect growing public disenchantment with the way their governments have handled a series of high profile crises which have now become part of the reality of the global age. Terrorist attacks perpetrated by non-state actors or financial crises resulting from market failures (and massive system-wide fraud) may originate in one part of the world, but they can briskly spread from one country to the next, producing devastating effects that are often deeply felt at the national and local levels. Reflecting a view that their governments 'did not do enough to protect them' or respond effectively afterwards, public attitudes towards government have grown increasingly negative. Though often originating well beyond their jurisdictional scope and control, citizens often find it politically convenient, and often personally consoling, to place the blame for such cataclysmic events on 'government bureaucrats' who, in their view, were 'asleep at the wheel'. Awkwardly, the massive cleanup often required in the aftermath of these events often falls on the shoulders of financially ever-strapped public authorities.

When politics and administration collide

A defining characteristic of both the field and practice of contemporary public administration involves the perpetually vexing question of where the politics of decision-making should end and where the politically neutral business of management and administration should take over. When the world of politics collides with administrative processes it can make for some intriguing drama. One of the most striking illustrations of this can be seen in a recent high stakes political face-off. On 1 October 2013, the world watched in bewilderment as for the first time in almost two decades the US government shut down. Resulting from a political impasse between the country's top political leaders in reaching a critical budget deal, the dramatic ordeal threatened to place the country's entire federal civil administration in limbo. Nearly one million public sector jobs were on the line as national parks, most federal offices, and the country's space programme were forced to close their doors. The negative fallout extended into the private sector as estimates surfaced suggesting that the closure was costing the economy nearly $300 million a day in lost productive output, threatening to imperil the country's fragile economic recovery from the recent global financial crisis.

The seeds of the budget standoff were not planted in the administrative process itself but rather in a fierce political battle that was being waged by the country's two major political parties over the decision to raise the debt ceiling in order to cover the massive $33 billion shortfall in the 2014 budget. In the absence of decisive action, speculations began mounting that the American government would default on its sovereign debt obligations. Many feared that an extended showdown would ignite a firestorm of investor panic that would cause a meltdown of the entire global financial system. Investor fears were confirmed when Standard & Poor's, one of the most respected credit assessment agencies, lowered America's sovereign debt rating, potentially limiting the country's ability to borrow more money. With each passing day of the standoff, faith in the country's leadership and administrative capacity eroded.

How could it come to this? Politically speaking, there was plenty of finger pointing on both sides of the partisan aisle. Right-of-centre political party leaders in the legislature blamed the country's runaway debt problem on what they perceived to be the massive spending appetite of President Barack Obama and his left-leaning

Box 1 America's healthcare exchange

In 2010 American lawmakers passed the politically contentious Affordable Care Act (ACA). The historic Act established 'Health Insurance Exchanges' in 2013 that serve as marketplaces for consumers to purchase health insurance from a range of federally certified private vendors. The Act also allows states the option to establish their own exchanges, establish regional cooperatives with other states, or partner with the Federal government. The processes involved in setting up and managing healthcare enrolment websites posed enormous challenges for state administrators. During the initial phase of their launch, five of the fourteen states that set up their own health exchanges were projected to spend nearly a quarter of a billion dollars to fix problems embedded in the enrolment websites.

political supporters. Opposition leaders viewed the budget standoff as an opportunity to negotiate for deep cuts in social spending. Meanwhile the American president accused his political opponents of holding the budget process hostage in a conspiratorial effort to defund the country's historic Affordable Care Act, popularly known as 'Obamacare' (see Box 1). While a tenuous budget compromise was ultimately reached and a full-blown crisis averted, the sixteen-day standoff illustrates the extent to which party-based politics is inextricably connected with the policy and administrative process. It further illustrates how destructive partisan politics can disrupt an entire national administrative system.

Should government be run like a business?

Mounting political demands for 'austerity' in government spending have compelled public agencies to take on new mandates, functions, and tasks in the face of diminishing financial resources. In other words, public agencies at all levels are being forced to do 'more with less'. The insatiable quest for 'leaner and meaner' forms of public governance has compelled policymakers and public sector managers across national, regional, and municipal arenas to shift their emphasis increasingly from process-based practices towards 'economically rationalized' outcomes. Within the last thirty years, for example, public administrators have been challenged to adapt their processes and service delivery methods in order to meet quantitatively measured targets such as cost–benefit analysis and other performance-based benchmarks. Indeed, a major source of tension in public administration involves an ongoing conflict between the democratic values of 'equity' and 'equality', and the market values of 'performance' and 'efficiency'.

Negative attitudes towards the public sector are reflected through the growing sentiment that 'government is the problem and not the solution'. Such sentiments have inspired the popular mantra that 'government should be run like a business'. One of the leading vanguards of this movement was British prime minister (1979–90), Margaret Thatcher. Thatcher believed that the growth of public spending in Britain was largely attributed to the 'uncontrollable' growth of government. Consequently she loathed the idea of increasing taxes to finance bloated state bureaucracies. The view that the private sector 'does it better' is shared by Britain's current prime minister, David Cameron, who recently stated that 'outside of the area of national security public services should be open to a range of providers competing to offer a better service'. While the joint activities of government and business are essential to a well-functioning society, applying the business logic of efficiency (in order to maximize profitability) to the public sector fails to acknowledge that the purpose and function of each of the two sectors are fundamentally distinct. Simply put, the public sector exists to provide 'public goods' or those services society as a whole pays for and from which no one can be excluded. This includes such indispensable items as public education and public highways. The private sector, by way of contrast, provides goods and services that are privately sold and consumed by individuals in the marketplace.

Questioning the appropriateness of applying business rationales to the public sector, economist John T. Harvey argues that 'not everything that is profitable is of social value and not everything of social value is profitable'. Harvey brings out, for example, that while many privately sold and consumed items, such as reality television or pornography, may be highly profitable in the private marketplace, they provide little social value in contributing to a well-functioning society. On the other hand, essentials such as military defence, public safety, and universal education often provide enormous social value without netting immediate cash returns to the citizens who pay for them.

Under the appropriate circumstances, the public sector may adopt certain private-sector-based management strategies and practices with great success. However, one must keep in mind that government agencies and the public administrators who serve in them, unlike businesses, must be accountable to those with a much wider set of constituent interests, and they are overseen by other governmental agencies. Therefore, handing over control of public sector processes and services (see Box 2), such as the management of the department of motor vehicle records or official court documents, to the private sector for file processing and storage management can potentially compromise citizens' privacy rights. Moreover, outsourcing these essential functions to private hands can move them beyond the scope of democratic accountability and oversight.

United in their contempt for the public sector and its historic mission of redistributing wealth through progressive taxation in order to fund social services, America's Tea Party leaped onto the national scene in 2009 with a bellicose anti-government campaign directed against Obama's 'big government' economic

Box 2 The Railtrack privatization debacle

The popular sentiment that 'the private sector is always more efficient than the public sector' is countered by some high profile botched privatizations. Publicly run British Rail, for instance, was split up and sold on the cheap to private investors in the 1980s. Under the new arrangement, the private firm Railtrack oversaw the track, signals, and station operations, while passenger service was assumed by twenty-eight separate companies. The privatization formula involved breaking up an integrated publicly run transportation network into more than a hundred separate private companies and subcontractors. As a result, Britain was left with a highly fragmented system which failed to provide essential supervision over vital traffic safety equipment. This resulted in a series of catastrophic collisions, which ultimately left thirty people dead and nearly 400 more injured.

recovery package and national healthcare scheme. The group included members belonging to the so called 'right-wing' of the Republican Party such as senators Jim DeMint of South Carolina and Ted Cruz of Texas as well as Congressional representatives such as Michele Bachmann of Minnesota and Marsha Blackburn of Tennessee. Soon after it appeared, anti-government populist movements with varying agendas began sprouting up around the globe. Ranging from 'hard right' to more extreme fascist movements, examples include the UK's Independence Party (UKIP), Germany's Alternative for Germany (AfD), and Greece's Golden Dawn.

Public administration and global turbulence

As we discussed earlier, global climate change and global terrorism are posing enormous challenges for public administrators operating at every level of government. Local public administrators in countries all over the world must be adept at managing crises that have originated outside their borders. Rapid global industrialization and urbanization, which appear to go hand in hand, have posed historic challenges for local public administrators, compelling them to expand their scope of responsibilities and areas of expertise. Indeed, many of the world's leading metropolitan areas are confronting major administrative dilemmas posed by untenable surges in urban density and urban sprawl. Public administrators are challenged to come up with effective solutions as existing infrastructure and civic resources are quickly being overwhelmed. Rising levels of carbon-based industrial pollution associated with aggressively expanding global production have been linked with recent increases in both the frequency and intensity of climate-change-related natural disasters. These events, in turn, have been wreaking havoc on large municipal areas, creating massive dilemmas for local administrators.
Let us look briefly at a few examples of how some of the forces associated with globalization have been affecting local public administration.

In the United States, municipal administrators are mandated as the first responders to any natural disaster or threat to public safety. When essential coordination and communication among national and local administrators is wanting during a crisis or emergency, the results can be catastrophic, as evidenced by the administrative debacle that followed in the wake of the natural disaster known as Hurricane Katrina. In the summer of 2005, what began as a Category One hurricane miles out to sea quickly transformed into a 125-mile-an-hour force of nature that ravaged the Southern Louisiana coast. Unrelenting rainfall and extreme winds battered the surrounding areas of the city of New Orleans, leaving 80 per cent of the municipal area under water (see Figure 1). While most urban neighbourhoods had been successfully evacuated before the hurricane made landfall, many residing in the outlying rural parishes were left behind to fend for themselves. As water levels continued to rise, adjacent canal levees began overflowing, eventually giving way and adding perilously to the

1. New Orleans underwater.

deluge. With water levels reaching as high as 15 feet in some areas, local, state, and federal administrators and officials quickly realized that relief plans and resources currently in place were grossly insufficient. When the hurricane itself finally subsided and the waters began to recede, the damage was surveyed. Bone-chilling estimates revealed the sobering reality: almost 300 lives had been lost in the initial disaster and many more people would die in the subsequent flooding or while waiting for help that never arrived. Millions more were injured, displaced, or left homeless. There were billions of dollars in property damage.

As the world would soon witness, however, the real tragedy lay in a massively botched emergency response effort that would come to symbolize 'government ineffectiveness' and 'incompetence'. Indeed, a 2006 government report would later confirm that 'federal, state, and local officials' failure to anticipate the post-landfall conditions delayed post-landfall evacuation and support'. Confusing guidelines distinguishing a 'normal disaster' from a 'catastrophe' coincided with the failure of officials at all levels to identify and communicate the severity of the flooding. Confusion and poor communication delayed the implementation of critical evacuation measures for almost twenty-four hours after the levees had been breached. Leading public administration expert Donald Kettl later remarked that 'when faced with Katrina, government at all levels failed' and that 'the bungled response ranks as perhaps the biggest administrative failures in American History'.

Virtually all communication service was knocked out in the flooding, leaving administrators and relief agents operating at multiple levels of government without any means of talking to one another on the ground for nearly four days. Even worse, no contingency protocols had been put in place in the event that the main lines should fail. The country's Federal Emergency Management Agency (FEMA) director, Michael Brown, was left out of discussions between the state's governor's office and the city mayor's office. Meanwhile, the chief of the Homeland Security

Department, Michael Chertoff, failed to provide the Bush administration with 'adequate advice and counsel' on how to proceed, thereby delaying federal assistance. Hurricane Katrina provides a classic example of how a natural disaster, coupled with administrative folly, ultimately could culminate in a historic catastrophe. Public outrage resulted in a fundamental rethinking of the nation's emergency relief process. Subsequent disaster relief efforts would involve substantial improvements in the level of coordination between various administrative agencies.

Let us now look at how overcrowding in some of the world's largest cities associated with global industrialization is creating confounding challenges for local government administrators across the world. Massive industrial urban-based growth in India, for example, has been a mixed blessing for the country. On the one hand, this has contributed to a substantial increase in the country's overall gross domestic product, while on the other, it has generated administrative nightmares for public officials in cities like Mumbai who have been unable to successfully manage the massive levels of sewage and solid waste that are being generated daily by that city's thirteen million residents. Dramatic images depicting life for the millions living in urban slums provide us with a glimpse of the intractability of the growing problem.

Urban planners in Shanghai, China, are working feverishly to address the epic urban density challenges posed by massive waves of migrant workers who have been steadily pouring into cities from rural areas in search of industrial employment (see Figure 2). So-called 'satellite towns', which have been springing up around major urban centres like Beijing, have been absorbing some of the growth, thereby easing some of the pressure on the municipal centres. However, an unrelenting stream of new residents in those areas is quickly overburdening existing utilities and transportation facilities. Even China's more remote cities have been experiencing population explosions of their

2. Urban density challenges.

own. With an exponentially growing population, the relatively obscure southwestern city of Kunming, for example, stands to overtake in population size some of America's largest cities within the next few years. Turning our attention to the southern hemisphere, Melbourne's civic officials, business leaders, and urban planners are struggling to address the new infrastructure and social service needs of its ever-growing population which is expected to balloon to an estimated five million residents by 2025 and almost six and a half million by 2050. Fuelled by new waves of immigrants pouring in from all over the world, especially Asia, Melbourne's population is expected to grow by 1,200 residents a week for the next four decades, requiring major planning initiatives to address new demands placed on the city's education, health, water, and transportation facilities. According to the Property Council of Australia, these new requirements are expected to include an 'extra 10,000 childcare spots by 2025 and 29,000 by 2050, about 3350 new hospital beds by 2025 and 8600 by 2050 and 5700 new classrooms by 2025 and 10,000 by 2050'.

As we can already see, public administration is a highly complex and dynamic subject that is interconnected with modern life. At the same time, we have only scratched the surface at this point in our story. Returning to the question raised by the prospective student at the outset of this chapter, we might say that public administration is the intersection of politics, policy, and management, and concerns the design and adoption of government policies and programmes. Most importantly, it involves the management and leadership required to carry them out. Stated simply, public administration encompasses the wide range of political and management processes required to implement 'public policy' in the real world. As we continue our tour we will explore the relationship between public administration as both a professional practice and a related academic discipline. As we shall see in the further pages of this volume, the two are inextricably related, highly fluid, and dynamic. The academic field is devoted to teaching public managers how to improve functions and operations of government organizations in carrying out their mandates. The goal of those teaching public administration is to help public managers hone their critical thinking skills in ways that will make them worthy 'custodians of the public trust'. Indeed, democracy depends on it.

That said, before one can begin to grasp the role that public administrators play in today's complex world one must attempt to understand the evolution of the modern state and the ever-shifting roles and functions of the public sector within it. The access to virtually unlimited sources of information at breakneck Internet speeds has empowered citizens to think and question what public servants do in their name. While questions may abound over who should be responsible for ensuring the quality and accuracy of this information, the notion of 'transparency' is fuelling hopes for the expansion of democratic accountability where it exists and its extension to areas where it has not yet taken root. The management of globally sourced information is presenting major challenges for public administrators.

Public sector agencies across the globe have been responding to these new imperatives by searching for innovative ways to increase their organizational 'capacity'. Consequently, today's public administrator is compelled to adopt flexible strategies and practices to cope with ever-changing political and economic landscapes. In many public agencies, new broods of highly skilled 'public sector professionals' are being groomed to replace the old image of the 'bureaucrat'. As a result, it should come as no surprise that student enrolments in public administration programmes are exploding in places like the US, Britain, Europe, and all the way to China and Australasia.

Chapter 2
The journey from Westphalia to Philadelphia

Let us now continue with a historical overview of the Anglo-American administrative traditions that have shaped contemporary administrative systems. As we shall explore in greater depth, 'public' administration, as distinct from other forms of civil administration, is interconnected with democratic governance. Before examining these administrative traditions, however, let us begin with a brief discussion of the foundations of the modern state and the emergence of 'popular sovereignty'.

The origins of contemporary governance and administration are popularly attributed to the birth of the modern state that emerged with the Peace of Westphalia in 1648. Ushering to a close the devastating Thirty Years' War (1618–48), which had consumed most of the central continent of Europe, the terms of the Westphalian Treaty established new, internationally recognized territorial borders and gave newly created sovereign states the legitimate right to govern their peoples and lands. Under their sovereign authority, states could establish new centralized administrative systems, standards, and protocols for managing domestic and international affairs.

The political philosophy underpinning modern democratic administrative systems in countries such as Britain, the United States, France, and India is rooted in the notion of 'popular sovereignty'. Presupposing that legitimate rule depends upon the 'consent of the people' (or consent of the governed), popular sovereignty and democracy are now often seen to go hand-in-hand. The seeds of popular sovereignty were planted with the English Civil War (1642–9) which resulted in the deposition of England's reigning King Charles I. Upon Charles I's death, England was declared to be a 'commonwealth' and placed under the supreme rule of the House of Commons for several years.

In large part because of the painful events that were first unleashed in 1642, the English philosopher, Thomas Hobbes, detested civil wars and the anarchy that he believed naturally followed. Hobbes reasoned that political and social stability within society depended upon the united rule of strong sovereign authorities. Accordingly, he argued, a regime's legitimacy extended from its ability to maintain political unity and secure a lasting peace. In 1651 Hobbes completed his most famous work *Leviathan*, in which he emphasized the importance of securing political and social order through a social contract. Under this arrangement, citizens collectively agreed to the rule of a sovereign central authority. A royalist, Hobbes argued that monarchies were best suited to these purposes. While (to Hobbes' delight) the English monarchy would eventually be restored, its sovereign power would be curtailed.

The slow journey toward popular sovereignty would continue with the Glorious Revolution of 1688. From then on, legal and administrative authority governing matters of taxation, royal appointments, war, ceremonial expenditures, and government budgets were transferred from the sovereign domain of the monarchy to the parliament. In this process, parliament would assume the major administrative functions of government. No longer subject to the 'arbitrary' and 'capricious' rule of an absolute monarch, these revolutionary institutional changes would create a greater sense of legitimacy and predictability in governmental decisions. These historic events, in turn, would ultimately help shape the democratic character that public administration would assume in the century to come. Indeed, while Britain is formally a constitutional monarchy, norms and institutions of representative governance are firmly embedded in its political system.

Asserting that an absolute monarchy was incompatible with a justly governed civil society, the enlightenment thinker John Locke provided a provocative justification for revolution that would help lend credence to the notion of popular sovereignty. In his *Second Treatise of Government*, published in 1690, Locke made a sound case for limited government. Presupposing that all legitimate governments derived their authority from the implied consent of the people, Locke claimed that all men possessed natural rights, independent of the laws of any particular ruler or regime. Indeed, Locke insisted that 'the purpose of government' was to protect 'life', 'liberty', and 'property'.

Locke's philosophical views were arguably shaped by his own career as a public administrator. The prolific philosopher assumed a number of administrative positions, which included a diplomatic post in France, a position as the secretary to the Council of Trade, and a position of commissioner of trade and plantations in America. Locke believed that politically impartial administrators must govern within the rule of law in order to ensure that the interests of the people and the 'common good' were being served. At the same time, however, Locke was keenly aware that civil servants should be free to operate with some degree of administrative discretion and autonomy when carrying out their functions and mandates.

The early traditions of American public administration

Locke's ideas on limited government and popular sovereignty would influence both the American Revolution and the US Constitution. Upon gaining their independence from Britain, the

Americans preserved many of the ideas and traditions of English law, public governance, and administration. Indeed, Thomas Jefferson drew inspiration from Locke's philosophical arguments when drafting America's Declaration of Independence. Similarly, James Madison leaned on Locke's views of limited government and social contracts when framing the US Constitution a decade later. In turn, as we shall now see, Jefferson's and Madison's respective views on the role of government and administrative power would ultimately shape distinct administrative traditions that prevail today.

Public administration scholar Donald Kettl provides a lucid overview of the so-called Hamiltonian, Jeffersonian, and Madisonian traditions and explains their relevance to contemporary discussions and debates concerning public administration and civic governance. Acknowledging that a government strong enough to protect citizens' 'inalienable' rights was also powerful enough to strip them away, the founders sought to strike the correct balance between administrative efficiency and individual liberty. Consequently, they wrestled with administrative proposals that would promote effective government, on the one hand, while attempting to place strict constitutional limits on its power, on the other. They became embroiled in a protracted debate, which continues to this day, over how best to ensure public accountability.

Due to his strongly-held beliefs in the need for centralized (federal) national power, Hamilton was identified with a political faction that would become known as the 'Federalists'. Suspicious of centralized national power and fervently supportive of the sovereign rights of subnational authorities, Jefferson was identified with a rival faction known as the 'Anti-Federalists'. Falling somewhere in the middle between the Jeffersonian and Hamiltonian perspectives on governance and administration is the Madisonian tradition. Let us briefly examine each of these traditions in a little more depth.

Emphasizing the need to separate political and administrative powers among discrete institutions in order to prevent the abuse of political authority, Madison adopted the system known as 'checks and balances'. It involved separating national governmental power among three coequal branches of government: executive (president), legislative (legislature), and judicial (courts). The legislative branch was largely responsible for creating the laws, the executive branch administered the laws, and the courts adjudicated the laws. In actuality, however, the powers assigned to the three branches of government were partly blended so that no one branch could exert inordinate power over another. Any president who attempted to usurp too much power, for example, could be impeached by the legislative branch and removed from office. Similarly if the legislature were to enact laws that were deemed offensive to the Constitution, the nation's highest court could overturn them. In most instances, both the legislative branch and the executive branch had to reach a political consensus in order to enact a law.

In order to preserve the balance of power between the presidency and the US Congress, Madison's Constitutional design was set up in a manner that created a permanent sense of tension between these branches of government. The Madisonian system typically forces policymakers and administrators to reach broadly-supported political consensuses in order to get anything done. To be sure, this process often involves protracted negotiations and long-fought compromises, making policy and administrative change slow and frustrating. In extreme instances, these tensions can evolve into intense and destructive conflicts. We saw one prominent example of this in our opening chapter with the 2013 budget standoff between President Obama and his partisan opponents in Congress. As the reader will recall, the failure of the executive and legislative branches to reach a budget compromise in that instance imperilled the entire global economy. When analysing the American system of checks and balances, however, it is important to keep in mind that Madison's focus was directed toward minimizing the threat of tyranny rather than maximizing administrative expediency.

Contrastingly, adherents of the so-called 'Hamiltonian' approach advocated a strong 'federal' government that would inspire national unity and create a distinct American political identity. Hamilton believed that a strong and relatively autonomous executive was essential to a well-functioning administrative system in order to get things done. In the collection of essays known as the *Federalist Papers*, Hamilton argued that a powerful executive would best ensure national security and domestic tranquillity as well as promote consistency in the administration of laws. In one essay, Hamilton argued, assertively, that 'a feeble executive implies a feeble execution of the government. A feeble execution is but another phrase for a bad execution: And a government ill executed, whatever it may be in theory, must be in practice a bad government.'

Having advocated a more hierarchical top–down approach to administrative governance, Hamilton and his band of Federalists became associated with the expansion of strong national government and hence were viewed as potential enemies of states' rights. Hamilton saw America as a potential industrial power that would ultimately challenge Britain's hegemony throughout the world. To accomplish his vision, Hamilton looked to the central government to finance the industrial growth of the country. Toward that end, Hamilton later used his administrative power as the country's first treasury secretary to establish the first Bank of the United States in order to consolidate the nation's revolutionary war debts and stabilize its currency. In attempting to centralize control over the country's finances, Hamilton further extended the power of the national government.

An outspoken critic of large-scale government, Jefferson distrusted centralized authority. Indeed, he envisioned a republic whereby political and administrative power was largely reserved for the states. Less focused on building the country into a major industrial power, Jefferson concentrated instead on providing states with the flexibility and autonomy to pursue their distinct destinies. While Hamilton believed in the virtues of strong executive power, Jefferson feared the potential for tyranny that might accompany vesting too much governing power and authority in a single administrative office. Guided by his natural mistrust of a strong monarch-like executive, Jefferson sought to entrust the nation's sovereign power to a more widely representative institution. Accordingly, Jefferson pressed for a strong legislative body where the states and their discrete interests would be adequately represented in the national policymaking and administrative decision-making process.

Proclaiming the virtues of limited government, Jefferson's followers insisted that government was a necessary evil to be viewed with suspicion and hence tempered through the rule of law. The Jeffersonian tradition became associated with bottom–up democracy where subnational state governments enjoyed wide latitude to adopt policies and apply them in ways that were consistent with local norms and customs. However, Jeffersonians sometimes overlooked the propensities for widespread political corruption in local governance and administration. Indeed, the Jeffersonian era would become associated with the birth of the spoils system whereby public employment and government services were administered on the basis of political patronage rather than equity and fairness. Indeed, by the time Jefferson completed his terms in office, nearly two-thirds of the government positions within his administration had been awarded to members of his own political party. The practice of appointing party supporters to federal administrative posts was often rationalized as 'responsive government'.

Ironically, Jefferson was perhaps among the least Jeffersonian presidents. Immediately upon assuming the presidency in 1801, he distinguished himself as more of a Hamiltonian executive leader. During his time in office, the size and power of the US federal government increased dramatically. With the Louisiana Purchase from Napoleonic France in 1803, Jefferson's administration oversaw the acquisition of nearly 800,000 square miles of territory. Financed largely by London's Barings Bank, the $23 million purchase represented one of the largest and most lucrative 'land grabs' in history. The massive acquisition would ultimately result in the addition of thirteen new states to the union. As growing numbers of people settled across the West, federal administrative agencies, such as the Federal Post Office, needed to be expanded significantly. Naturally, the size of government and the scope of executive power grew in tandem with the new administrative system. One well-known historian, Henry Adams, asserted that Jefferson wielded executive power 'more complete than had ever before been known in American history'. Sympathetic to the idea that empires require emperors to run them, many Hamiltonians quietly approved.

Jefferson assumed office with the intent of reducing the size of government and the country's public debt. Having inherited nearly $83 million in public debt from his predecessors (largely left over from the revolutionary war), Jefferson was immediately compelled to modify his small-government agenda. Moreover, his administration was later forced to borrow an additional $15 million in order to complete the Louisiana Purchase. Convinced that the modest number of civilian administrators serving in the federal government were indispensable to the service of the country, Jefferson looked elsewhere for the necessary cuts. Strongly opposing the proposition that the nation should maintain domestic peace and security by preparing for war, Jefferson made substantial cuts in the country's military expenditures. With these large cuts, a booming economy resulting from territorial expansion, and increases in tariffs on goods consumed by the rich, Jefferson's administration ultimately reduced the nation's debt by nearly 60 per cent.

Reflections for contemporary public administration

Contemporary debates over the proper size and scope of government and administrative power reflect (whether directly or indirectly) the core issues outlined in the Hamiltonian and Jeffersonian traditions. Consistent with Jefferson's reasoning that local governments are more representative of the character of the people, and hence more likely to be responsive to their concerns, political movements have urged the devolution of centralized sovereign political power and administrative authority to subnational governments.

Growing numbers of citizens in the United Kingdom have been pressing for greater political decentralization in certain areas of the country. In response to citizens' demands for more direct representation and greater political autonomy, a series of steps have been undertaken by the British Parliament to confer greater administrative and political authority to the Scottish National Parliament, the National Assembly of Wales, and the Northern Ireland Assembly. On 18 September 2014, a much anticipated referendum was held to determine whether or not to make Scotland an independent country. While 55 per cent of the electorate voted in favour of maintaining the status quo, significant numbers of citizens continue to feel very strongly that Scotland should be granted independence.

Arguing on the grounds that the particular needs and cultural values of citizens in Mississippi and South Carolina are radically different from those in New York and California, many local politicians and citizens have been pressing for greater states' rights. Again, as we saw in the opening chapter, Tea-Party-like groups in the US have been demanding that state governments be granted complete control over policy issues ranging from educational curriculum reform and reproductive rights to gun control and illicit drug use.

Public servants and citizens alike will continue to grapple with administrative dilemmas resulting from conflicts shaped by contending perspectives on governance. In recent years, the states of Colorado, Washington, Oregon, and Alaska have legalized the use of marijuana, while the US federal government and many other states have not. Naturally, this has created widespread confusion among public administrators and the multiple agencies involved in drug enforcement. Under the current jurisdictional division, for example, citizens may possess and use marijuana in the greater Denver metropolitan area. However, if a citizen should enter onto the physical premises of the Denver International Airport, which operates under the national airport authority, he/she may be charged with a federal crime. As we shall see in subsequent pages, administrative tensions between national and local jurisdictions will grow increasingly complex in the global age.

Chapter 3
Progressive reform across the globe

'Modern', 'rationally structured', hierarchical state administrative bureaucracies coincided with the centralization of government authority and the expansion of European imperialist military systems in the 18th and 19th centuries. By the early 1700s the Prussian Empire boasted a highly complex and well-defined administrative apparatus that extended into both military and civil affairs. In Britain, modern elements of civil bureaucracy owe some credit to the officers and agents employed in the East India Company. Initially established in 1600 as a private holdings firm under a Royal Charter, the company later evolved into a political and economic power. In so doing, it established auxiliary civil administrative offices and an elaborate military command structure. Indeed, this system would later be assumed by the British Empire to govern vast parts of the subcontinent. The consolidation of regional territories under the political authority and military protection of 'nation-states' that emerged in the 19th century supported the expansion of hierarchically structured administrative systems. The consolidation of France under Napoleon, the solidification of the 'American nation' following the Civil War of 1865, the unification of 'Italy' under Giuseppe Garibaldi in 1860–70, and the rise of a new Germany in 1871 under Bismarck were important developments.

While the characteristics and dimensions of the 'modern nation-state' continue to be debated among political scientists and historians, as we shall see in the following pages, they helped lay the foundations not only of the modern field and practice of public administration but also of modern social welfare systems in America and Western Europe. Public administrators were compelled, consequently, to adopt new 'bureaucratic' methods and processes to carry out their new functions and mandates. As we shall see, these new administrative processes were rooted in principles and methods that were associated with the so-called 'Gilded Age' and the 'Scientific Revolution'. Let us first discuss the American progressive era and then explore the progressive reforms that would ultimately shape European welfare states.

America

As we discussed in Chapter 2, the widespread practice of doling out administrative favours and public services in exchange for votes initially surfaced during the Jeffersonian era. As the geography and population of the country continued to increase into the next century, a vigorous public sector blossomed. The presidential election of 1824 and the ascension to power of Andrew Jackson were tethered to an emergent populist movement comprised of small farmers in the American South and industrial workers in the North. Claiming to represent the 'plain people', Jackson pursued a more inclusive form of democracy. This involved an extension of the voting franchise to growing numbers of people, representing a broadened spectrum of social and economic classes. Proclaiming that the country's political processes and administrative system had long been captured by the country's elite farmers (known as 'plantocrats'), big businessmen, and wealthy bankers, Jackson embraced a populist agenda that was meant to appeal to a more diverse group of voters.

Under 'Jacksonian Democracy', as it would later be known, political party candidates were nominated through formal conventions that were held in the open rather than chosen in secret by party elites behind closed doors. As America's electoral processes became more accessible to growing numbers of people, traditionally underrepresented social classes entered the political fray. Political candidates extended the practice of offering political favours and expanding the scope of public services in order to win the support of an ever-growing and diverse electorate. 'Machine politics' were embedded in every level of political life. New York City's infamous Tammany Hall and its corrupt mayor, 'Boss' William M. Tweed, ran one of the most well-oiled political machines of that era. 'Manufacturing' votes in exchange for political patronage, Tammany Hall was praised by many for providing essential public services to otherwise underrepresented immigrants and working poor. At the same time, however, the nefarious mayor and his 'political cronies' in city hall were heavily criticized by others for their unscrupulous practices.

By the mid-1800s, increasing numbers of Americans, who were growing tired of the gross inequities produced under the spoils system, began demanding social protections and comprehensive civil service reform. Progressive leaders urged federal, state, and local governments to work together to implement new policies aimed at improving social justice and workplace conditions, especially in the country's industrial sector. These new policies and regulations included establishing a legal working age to protect children, limiting the number of hours in a working day, and enacting a variety of health and safety measures. In an effort to limit the oligopolistic control and manipulation of the free market by a few large corporations, progressives pushed Congress to pass the Sherman Anti-Trust Act of 1890.

The assassination of President James A. Garfield in 1881 marked the rise of the new administrative period known as the 'progressive era'. Progressives sought to replace inefficient governing practices associated with political patronage with professional standards that emphasized efficiency and equity. Related reforms were undertaken in the area of civil service employment. The adoption of the Pendleton Act in 1883, for example, led to the creation of a Civil Service Commission, which attempted to secure greater fairness and transparency in public sector hiring and promotion. The Pendleton Act created new processes and mandates that eventually helped put an end to many spoils practices. By the turn of the century, the vast majority of federal jobs in the civil service sector were appointed and overseen through a strict merit system. Consequently, the growing demand for 'well-trained' and 'professionally qualified' bureaucrats dramatically changed the practice of public administration.

Some progressive leaders sought to develop a new professional field that would explore innovative administrative methods and techniques for improving bureaucratic functions and operations. One of the leading pioneers in this movement was Woodrow Wilson. Often described as the 'father of the field of public administration', Wilson believed that the political and administrative spheres of governance should be separate and mutually exclusive. Wilson contended that politics was the domain of special interests while public administration existed to serve the public interest. Wilson argued that the functions of public services should be administered in a manner consistent with the highest professional standards and codes of ethics. He further believed that public servants should be insulated from the corrupting influence of partisan politics and political patronage. Wilson argued that politics should be limited to matters related to policy formulation and adoption and that public administration should be devoted exclusively to the 'detailed and systematic execution of public law'.

Wilson became a prominent voice in the academic discipline of political science. Wilson's new 'science' would be devoted to the study of 'those deep and permanent principles of politics' that were established over the past two millennia and had since become embedded within the cultural and normative fabric of democracy. Leading public administration scholars, such as Frank Goodnow, joined the discourse by raising important questions about where the politics of decision-making should end and where the neutral business of management and administration should begin. Scholars like Wilson and Goodnow sought to incorporate organizational management ideas and systems into the public sector practice. The new interdisciplinary field ultimately drew on many sources, including the methods of organizational efficiency emphasized by the school on scientific management led by American engineer Frederick Winslow Taylor and German sociologist Max Weber's principles of rational bureaucracy.

Taylor stressed the importance of standardizing work methods and streamlining production processes to reduce waste and improve labour productivity. In his groundbreaking book, *The Principles of Scientific Management*, Taylor emphasized the use of systematic analysis and formal engineering methods to study worker performance and workflow processes, so as to improve their function and operation. Applying scientific tools of empirical observation and rigorous metrics, he believed managers could discover the optimal method for performing any task. Taylor believed that once these methods were discovered, common best practices could be established and then applied elsewhere.

Taylor believed that each human being was unique and, therefore, possessed a distinct set of skills. Taylor asserted that it was important for management to identify each worker's personal strengths and assign the 'right person' to perform the 'right task'. He further claimed that organizations that paid their employees fair wages, and allowed them to take regularly scheduled breaks, achieved higher levels of worker satisfaction. These practices, in turn, would contribute to increased productivity. To be sure, many organizations selectively applied certain aspects of Taylorism while ignoring others. Taylor's principles were frequently applied incorrectly to compel employees to work harder. As a result, most of the responsibility for organizational performance was unduly placed on the workers.

As Taylor's principles began being embraced throughout government bureaucracies, growing numbers of public servants were held to strict accountability standards. In addition, Taylor's principles were introduced into municipal administration through the adoption of the commission and city manager systems. Municipal commissions were comprised of elected representatives who served as heads of city departments. Each department was responsible for overseeing specific areas under its jurisdiction such as public utilities, sanitation, and police. The city manager system was comprised of professional administrators who were recruited to manage and oversee the numerous functions and processes involved in municipal governance. Operating under formal business practices and organizational principles, city managers were responsible for overseeing the implementation of activities carried out by various municipal departments. These departments ranged from the city clerk's office to the planning and development bureau. Many of the principles underpinning 'classical organizational theory' that developed from the 1920s to 1950s were based upon Taylor's work. Indeed, Taylor's 'principles of scientific management' have continued to influence both the academic field and practice of public administration over the last sixty years.

Britain

One of the defining issues that has shaped British class politics since the 19th century has been the development and maintenance of the welfare state. Not unlike America, Britain travelled on a long, arduous, and at times pernicious path. Introduced during the Elizabethan era in 1601, the Poor Laws were adopted to formalize relief practices that were established to protect the indigent poor in England and Wales. Industrialization brought a variety of new social problems that needed to be systematically addressed. Over time, the provisions associated with the original Elizabethan laws had become a large financial burden on Britain's wealthier classes. By 1830, the costs associated with social assistance for the poor had risen to an estimated £7 million per year. As a result, specific reforms were adopted during the Victorian era that were intended to reduce some of these costs.

In the 19th century, harsh living and working conditions associated with mass industrial development took a heavy toll on the lives of large numbers of people. High levels of pollution and toxic compounds generated by London's bustling industrial sector posed serious health hazards for workers and their families. Overcrowding and pollution in urban areas were the leading causes of disease and poor health during this period. In order to manage the growing costs associated with caring for the sick and assisting the country's poor population, systematic reforms were adopted by parliament. Insisting that sound health practices contributed to 'good business', pro-business social reformers, such as Edwin Chadwick, pushed for major changes in this area. In response to growing public pressures, parliament passed the (new) Poor Law of 1834. This Act significantly reduced the costs of poor relief. Additional measures were adopted regulating dangerous industrial work practices and processes in mining and manufacturing. Most notably, the new Poor Law established shelters, known as workhouses, for the increasing numbers of unemployed workers and their families. In many instances families residing in these facilities were provided basic sustenance in the form of clothing, food, and rudimentary education. Although the facilities were originally intended to provide temporary relief, many tenants, faced with no other options, ended up staying for extended periods of time. Life was difficult for most residents. Countless able-bodied residents were required to perform 'hard labour' in exchange for receiving basic levels of assistance. Because of their harsh living conditions, some leading progressive activists of the day, such as Richard Oastler, regarded these workhouses as 'prisons for the poor'.

The Poor Laws of the early 1800s created further disparities between the middle classes and the working poor. This was partly because, in the absence of any systemic central administration and oversight, many of the services provided under the Act were unevenly (and sometimes inhumanely) administered at the discretion of local parishes. Public outrage over workhouse conditions and other provisional abuses led to the abolition of the Poor Law Commission which had been established to oversee the administration and operations associated with 1834 Poor-Law-related services. Further reform efforts attempted to address some of these issues.

In the spring of 1853, a comprehensive review of Britain's civil administration system was initiated under the oversight of William Gladstone, then chancellor of the exchequer. In the following year, a document that would become known as the Trevelyan-Northcote Report (named for its authors Charles Trevelyan and Stafford Northcote) recommended revolutionary changes to this system. Besides proposing that examinations be administered to ensure that prospective civil servants were adequately qualified, the report suggested that promotions be administered through a competitive and transparent merit system. According to Professor Peter Hennessy, the proposed reforms would be 'the greatest single governing gift of the nineteenth to the twentieth century: a politically disinterested and permanent Civil Service with core values of integrity, propriety, objectivity and appointment on merit, able to transfer its loyalty and expertise from one elected government to the next'.

From 1906 to 1914, a series of historic social welfare reforms were enacted under the leadership of the prime minister Herbert Asquith and chancellor of the exchequer David Lloyd George. In 1906, for example, the safety regulations outlined in the 1901 Factory Act were expanded to cover additional industries. In 1908, the Old Age Pensions Act was introduced which extended retirement benefits to those over 70 who had worked most of their adult life. Indeed, this Act helped establish the foundation for a broader set of progressive welfare reforms. One year later, the first labour exchanges were established to help unemployed workers find new jobs. That same year, the government enacted the Development Fund, which was designed to generate new employment through new infrastructure projects in areas ranging from agriculture to transport during recessionary periods. Perhaps the crowning achievement of this period, however, was the Asquith government's enactment of national health and unemployment insurance. The Act provided for a range of benefits including medical treatment for both physical and mental illnesses. Financed jointly through the contributions made by both workers and the state, unemployment insurance was extended to workers whose employment was highly susceptible to structural changes in the economy. One of the political masterminds behind these historic social welfare schemes was Lloyd George, who successfully saw them through parliament. In crafting England's National Insurance Act of 1911, as is widely documented, Lloyd George drew inspiration from his 1908 study of Bismarck's revolutionary insurance benefit schemes.

While revolutionary for their day, many of the reforms discussed earlier offered only limited coverage and protections to certain groups of people. Many workers who participated in the labour exchange programme, for example, were only successful in assuming part-time casual employment. Moreover, workers were required to pay their National Insurance contributions out of their own earnings. It is important to note, however, that within less than five years of its adoption, an estimated two million workers had national unemployment insurance, and millions more were covered by national health insurance. Perhaps even more importantly, despite their shortcomings and limitations, these progressive developments were pivotal in the evolution of the modern welfare state.

European progressivism

National identities in Western Europe became more pronounced and salient in the second half of the 1880s. The emergence of so-called European 'nation-states' profoundly affected the structure and scope of public administration. As we shall see, the relationship between strong central governments and local authorities was characteristically more harmonious than in America and Britain. Let us examine some of the structural differences that distinguish these administrative systems. Political scientist B. Guy Peters outlines three Western European administrative state traditions which include: the French or Napoleonic Continental European tradition; the Germanic or Organicist Continental European tradition; and the Scandinavian State tradition.

In Europe as in America, the mass urbanization associated with industrialization placed enormous stress on society and the social provisions designed to assist the working and indigent poor. While both Western European and American reform movements evolved in tandem with an increasingly democratic state, European progressives envisioned a much more paternalistic role for government. Consequently, Europeans looked to government to provide basic economic security for their citizens and viewed the state as the guarantor of prosperity for civil society as a whole. Similar to the American and British experience, progressive reforms undertaken in this era proved transformative in laying the foundation of modern welfare states.

France

In 1804, Napoleon Bonaparte sought to revamp France's entire political and administrative system in accordance with the 'enlightenment' ideals that inspired the French Revolution (1789–99). Napoleon attempted to consolidate the various provincial laws that had been developed discretely over the course of the country's feudal history into a modern and uniform civil code. With a highly centralized state bureaucracy, the lines between the 'state' and 'society' were not as pronounced as in the American system. Unlike the American system, where the national and state governments were constitutionally separated,

French administrative power was unified. The overarching principle behind the comprehensive reform of the country's legal system was to ensure that every French citizen was guaranteed equal protection under law. Once adopted, the code was applied universally across France and ultimately extended to citizens residing in all French territories and jurisdictions. Indeed, the Napoleonic tradition ultimately influenced the legal and administrative systems of various countries throughout Western Europe as well as parts of North Africa and the American South.

The extensive scope of the Napoleonic Code covered areas such as Civil Procedure (1804), Commercial Law (1807), Criminal Procedure (1808), and the Penal system (1810). The redesign of the administrative code in 1808, in particular, transformed the entire French civil service system. Encompassing everything from tax policy to banking and finance, the code created new administrative offices and established definitive lines of jurisdiction and accountability. There emerged, among much else, the Courts of Accounts, the General Inspection of the Finances, and the Council of State. Moreover, the Napoleonic period became associated with one of the most ambitious administrative public works programmes the world had ever seen. France's elaborate new administrative apparatus oversaw the construction and procurement of new canals, ports, and harbours, besides managing the expansion of a comprehensive road system that improved French access to other parts of Europe.

One of the leading architects of the Napoleonic administrative code was progressive theorist Charles-Jean Bonnin. In his book *Principes d'administration publique* (*Principles of Public Administration*), published in 1812, Bonnin outlined sixty-eight principles for administrative governance. The majority of these principles involved specific rules that administrative organizations ought to follow in order to operate more efficiently and responsibly. The principles applied to those serving in all levels of administration, from department ministers to street-level supervisors serving in

France's countless bureaucratic offices. Bonnin shared Wilson's view that 'administration' should be studied as a distinct set of practices and activities that set them apart from the political methods exercised by 'government' and the 'state'. Similarly, Bonnin's interdisciplinary approach jointly embraced the use of formal methodologies drawn from the natural sciences as well as concepts gleaned from the social sciences and humanities to improve the functions and activities associated with administrative governance.

In 1916, French mining engineer Henri Fayol introduced a revolutionary approach to public management that became known as 'administrative management theory'. In his book, *General Industrial Management*, Fayol outlined several important principles which reflected the actual complexities involved in managing large organizations. While 'Taylorism' emphasized the use of empirical science-based methods for improving worker efficiency and precision in the performance of specific tasks, Fayol's approach stressed management's role in shaping and defining organizational purposes. Fayol asserted that managers must assume responsibility for ensuring organizational success by setting objectives and cultivating unity among various divisions and departments through central coordination and control. Fayol believed that forecasting, planning, and training were essential elements in promoting organizational efficiency and workplace productivity. Fayol's principles were designed to be flexible and universally applicable to any organizational context.

Germany

In 1883, Germany's first chancellor, Otto von Bismarck, introduced a comprehensive progressive agenda. Building upon existing social programmes developed under Prussian and Saxon rule, Bismarck unveiled Europe's first social insurance scheme. By 1900 German workers were guaranteed healthcare coverage, a retirement pension, a minimum wage, vacation time, unemployment insurance, safe working conditions, and free childhood education. Initially adopted to satisfy the growing needs and demands of Germany's working class, these social schemes laid the foundation for the steady expansion of the social welfare system that remained in place until the Second World War.

As the role of government expanded with unification of the German states in the 1860s, a more professional administrative arm of government was required to manage and administer new social schemes and programmes. It was in this context that the German-Austrian school of public administration first emerged. One of the leading figures in this scholarly movement was Lorenz von Stein (1815–90). Stein adopted an interdisciplinary approach to the study of public administration that drew on diverse fields of human knowledge aimed at improving the practices of administrative governance. Through his extensive multi-volume exegesis entitled *The Theory of Administration (Die Verwaltungslehre)*, Stein attempted to elevate public administration to a 'systematic science'. In order to make the principles outlined in this 'major work' widely accessible to teachers and students, he later released his *Handbook of the Theory of Administration (Handbuch der Verwaltungslehre)*. Stein argued that the administrative activities of the state should be studied and analysed by examining areas such as domestic and international security, diplomacy, budget, and finance. He proposed that these distinct areas of study should be brought together under a single discipline to improve the internal workings of state administrative agencies in ways that serve the interests of the community and protect the rights of individual citizens.

The writings of German sociologist Max Weber transformed organizational theory and administrative science. As noted earlier, the industrial revolution and expansion of the state inspired the development of radically new organizational models. The need to coordinate complex operations and functions associated with large-scale public and private enterprises led to radical changes in their organizational structure. Weber's notion of bureaucracy was formulated from this context. Weber asserted that modern organizations needed to adopt rational bureaucratic processes and procedures based on formal rules, professional classification systems staffed with properly skilled, well-trained personnel, and well-structured divisions of labour. Under the Weberian model, professional bureaucrats were appointed and promoted within administrative positions based on their skill sets and levels of expertise. In order to perform highly specialized tasks and functions, bureaucrats were expected to receive professional training and education.

In his seminal works on bureaucracy, Weber mapped out key organizational principles that comprised his 'ideal' bureaucratic archetype. For Weber, bureaucracies were the instruments through which policy decisions were converted into concrete actions. The role of bureaucracies, therefore, was to ensure the effective implementation of government policies through impersonal, efficient, and standardized decision-making processes.

Weber did not view bureaucratic implementation as a democratic exercise. In fact, he believed that pluralistic forms of decision-making most often resulted in inconsistencies in the way policies were executed and implemented. Therefore, Weber argued that policy decisions should be implemented through authoritative decision processes using precise methods for execution. Under the Weberian model, policies and regulations, established under public law, were managed down though hierarchically organized offices and departments. Likewise, formal rules were enforced through a strict chain of command such that managers and workers reported to assigned supervisors.

Weber shrewdly observed that most policies developed by political officials rarely provided explicit language on the methods and means by which administrators should implement them. Rather, most statutes, he noted, were written in broad and often ambiguous language, giving administrative agencies, and public bureaucrats within them, wide latitude for interpreting when and how to carry them out. Weber asserted, therefore, that the actual power of bureaucracies rested in their ability to control the methods involved in the day-to-day implementation of public policies. Weber's principles have served to define the structure and role of the modern bureaucratic organization. Weber's 'ideal' bureaucratic model was characterized by a set of basic organizational principles which appear in Box 3.

> **Box 3 Weber's bureaucratic organizational principles**
>
> *Hierarchy of offices*: Institutional offices are arranged in a clear hierarchy; this allows for power and authority to be based upon a clear chain of command, with each office being supervised by a higher ranking office—thus allowing for disciplined implementation and ensuring bureaucratic authority.
>
> *Fixed division of labour*: Tasks in the bureaucratic organization are divided into functionally distinct areas each with requisite authority and sanction; essentially each office has a jurisdictional area that is clearly specified and governed by a set of duties and rights.
>
> *Rational-legal authority*: Formal roles and procedures ensure uniformity of implementation and regulation of bureaucratic behaviour; their authority stems entirely from their role and not from some private status, and their authority exists only as far as it is needed to carry out that role.
>
> *Impersonality*: Bureaucratic management is based on impersonally applied rules that are rational and allows for decisions made at the highest levels to be executed consistently by all lower levels; rules and controls are applied uniformly so as to prevent bureaucrats' personal preferences from dictating behaviour.

> **Box 3 Continued**
>
> *Appointment by qualification*: Appointments to bureaucratic positions are determined by tests of professional skill and competence, and not by considerations of status or patronage; employment and promotion are based upon merit, technical qualifications, competence, and performance.
>
> *Professionalism*: Bureaucrats are professional officials employed for a fixed salary; thus they do not own the units they manage.
>
> *Independent non-partisanship*: There is a distinct separation of the bureaucrats' personal beliefs and lives from their professional lives; administration is carried out on a continuous basis and not simply at the leadership's dictates based upon personal and ideological beliefs.
>
> *Sources*: Ken Johnson, 'According to Max Weber: historical principles' in 'Busting Bureaucracy'; Stella Z. Theodoulou and Christopher Kofinis, *The Art of the Game*, pp. 170–1.

Scandinavia

The Scandinavian tradition of public administration developed as a mixture of the Anglo-Saxon and Germanic traditions. In the early part of the 19th century, Sweden was one of the least industrially developed countries in Europe. The gap between the country's exclusive class of rich elites and large number of poor farmers was significant. However, as Sweden became industrialized and the country's wealth increased, the income gap between the rich and the poor narrowed considerably. Sweden was industrialized later than many of its European counterparts. As a result, some scholars have argued persuasively, the fierce tensions and intense class conflicts that developed between the rich land owners, industrialists, and working class groups in countries like Britain were not as pronounced. In European countries that industrialized relatively late, peasant and working class groups tended to be stronger and hence were received by other powerful economic classes as more equal partners. The mutual inclusion of diverse interests in shaping the political development of the Swedish nation-state in the 1800s resulted in the formation of cross-class coalitions of employers and workers. These developments helped shape the political culture and institutions through which national social policies developed. A substantial number of social services in Sweden are both organized and administered at the local level. This arrangement has helped foster a closer relationship between Swedish citizens and the public administrators who provide these public services. Moreover, the political tension between private business and the public sector has historically been less pronounced in Sweden than in its American and British counterparts.

By the mid-1800s Sweden was experiencing many of the painful effects associated with growing industrialization. One of the earliest social services introduced in 1842 by the Swedish state was compulsory elementary education. As the Swedish nation-state become firmly established in the late 1800s, employers and workers jointly supported the expansion of social insurance provisions that were provided by the national government.

The formation of the Swedish Social Democratic Labour Party (SAP) in 1889 was based on a progressive agenda that chiefly emphasized universal suffrage and an eight-hour work day. Though disagreements among moderates and more extreme leftists within the party would persist over how best to achieve these goals, there was general agreement on the ends. Moreover, the party's relatively modest progressive goals began gaining political traction among the country's mainstream electorate.

Responding to growing populist sentiments for social reform, the Swedish parliament passed important social insurance legislation in the years between 1891 and 1894. The Swedish government later provided extensive public services and public employment through a variety of tax-based cash benefit schemes. In 1882, new reform measures were adopted by Sweden's national government to eliminate the unfair tax burdens imposed on small-scale employers. The Act of 1913 extended flat-rate pension benefits to all Swedish citizens aged 67 and older. Established as part of a special First World War administration project in 1914, the National Unemployment Commission became the main administrative authority governing Swedish labour market policy for the next two decades. Its main purpose was to reduce unemployment by providing financial and administrative support for a variety of public works projects. In that same year, the Swedish national government began providing supplemental funds for poor relief programmes administered by local authorities.

The industrial revolution and the emergence of centralized nation-states in the second half of the 1800s dramatically transformed the relations between governments and societies. During this historic period, public services and welfare provisions increased by epic proportions. Citizens' expectations of government have grown considerably since the progressive era. Unemployment and social insurance, public transportation, and public parks and libraries were all products of democratic social movements. As the 20th century unfolded, societies continued to grow more complex, resulting in the development of additional public services and regulations. Consequently, the administrative processes and procedures involved in delivering these new government services became increasingly specialized and bureaucratic. In this process, governments assumed new responsibilities in protecting and promoting the economic and social security of citizens.

Chapter 4
The rise of the modern welfare state

Let us continue our exploration of the evolution of the public sector and the rise of the modern welfare state. The historical backdrop for our discussion begins with the devastating depression that swept across the globe in the late 1920s and early 1930s. Leaders in the industrialized countries watched helplessly as the value of their country's assets seemed to evaporate almost overnight. Meanwhile, national industries collapsed and millions of citizens found themselves unemployed and destitute. As we shall see, these terrible events would compel policymakers in Western democracies to develop new administrative systems and governing approaches.

Believed to have originated in the United States with the stock market crash of October 1929, the Great Depression quickly became the most pervasive economic crisis of the 20th century. Consumer spending and investment plummeted, causing steep declines in industrial output. As economic conditions worsened, countless workers were laid off. A massive deflation in the value of liquid assets caused capital markets to dry up. Befuddled governments hastily erected a series of protectionist policies in an attempt to shield their domestic markets from further international contagion. These measures mainly took the form of beggar-thy-neighbour policies such as tariffs on imports and currency devaluations. The adoption of these stop-gap remedies seemed to make the situation even worse. By the mid-1930s the world economy had plunged into a deep economic depression. The absence of any overarching administrative apparatus or coherent policy strategy resulted in massive gaps in the manner in which national relief provisions were administered among the people in the various countries that were affected. As growing numbers of citizens fell into further distress, Western governments faced intense political pressure to respond with drastic and permanent solutions.

While the precise causes of the global depression remained debatable, the economic ideas espoused by English economist John Maynard Keynes received wide attention. Keynes asserted that an economy moves in cycles, in very specific ways. He believed that aggregate output, and consequently employment, was a function of aggregate demand. He attributed rises in unemployment, therefore, to a shortage of private capital investment and spending in the economy. Keynes attributed this phenomenon to short-sighted privateers, whose investment decisions were often guided by irrational expectations and fears about future profitability. Negative expectations, he asserted, lead to declines in investment spending, thus bringing declines in demand and output, which cause unemployment to rise.

Keynes's ideas contributed substantially to the emergence of the field known as 'macroeconomics'. This new field shifted the focus from individual to the aggregate behaviour of economic actors in a country as a whole. Keynesian economists proceeded according to the belief that it was possible for national governments to collect and analyse large sets of economic data and predict crises prior to their occurrence. Armed with this knowledge, governments could then intervene in the economy by using specific sets of fiscal policy tools. For example, governments could increase public expenditures during the onset of economic recessions to help fuel growth, and reduce government expenditures when encountering economic booms in order to reduce pressures on inflation. Governments in Western industrialized countries later adopted a comprehensive set of new regulatory systems and policies aimed at preventing future crises.

The widespread application of Keynesian ideas by various governments across the industrialized world, ranging from the United States to Europe to Japan and Australia, led many to refer to the period from 1945 to the 1970s as 'the golden age of managed capitalism'. The American 'New Deal' and 'Great Society' programmes that were adopted under presidents Franklin D. Roosevelt (FDR) and Lyndon B. Johnson, the programmes of Swedish social democracy, and the welfare programmes introduced by the Labour Party in Britain from 1945 reflected a historic political consensus that was shared across Western democracies (Table 1). This period was characterized by the development of exchange rate regimes to promote stable international markets and the expansion of welfare states to protect labour and the working poor. Let us look at some of the conditions that influenced the rise of modern welfare states in specific countries.

In his book *Supercapitalism: The Transformation of Business, Democracy, and Everyday Life*, former United States Secretary of

Table 1 Year of introduction of various social services in selected nations

	Old-age pension	Unemployment insurance	Sickness pay	Medical services
Germany	1889	1927	1889	1883
Britain	1908	1911	1911	1911
Sweden	1913	1914	1914	1914–1946
United States	1935	1935		1965

Labor, Robert B. Reich, provides a lauding overview of the 'golden age of managed capitalism': 'The economy was based on mass production. Mass production was profitable because a large middle class had enough money to purchase what could be mass produced. The middle class had the money because the profits from mass production were divided among giant corporations and their suppliers, retailers, and employees. The bargaining power of this latter group was enhanced and enforced by government action. Almost a third of the workforce belonged to a union. Economic benefits were also spread across the nation—to farmers, veterans, small towns, and small business—through regulation (of railroads, telephones, utilities, and small business) and subsidies (price supports, highways, federal loans).'

Germany

Germany was one of the first nations to respond to the economic crisis of the 1930s with a series of spending initiatives for new programmes and projects directly aimed at ameliorating the country's rampant unemployment problem. In the years leading up to the war, however, the face of German welfare policy and the country's responses to the depression took a dramatic turn. Unemployment insurance, for example, was eliminated and replaced with a broader public works programme.

At the end of the war, Germany was divided into two separate states. West Germany was allied with the Western powers while East Germany became associated with the Eastern European Soviet bloc. These countries had radically different political and economic systems, as well as distinct administrative structures and welfare states. Whereas Eastern Germany adopted the Soviet-inspired command and control—centralized top–down—administrative model, West Germany adopted a more public-centric administrative system like that of most Western-style democracies.

Challenged with having to integrate large numbers of refugees, war veterans, and victims into society in the years immediately following the end of the war, West German leaders were compelled to both reconsider and reconstruct the country's entire social welfare system. Historic social welfare legislation was introduced as a major part of the nation's new constitution in 1949 known as 'The Basic Law'. The Basic Law guaranteed a host of social protections to each citizen through the establishment of a 'social state' (*Soziale Rechtsstaat*). In many respects, the administrative architecture was inspired by the 'Bismarckian welfare state' discussed in Chapter 3. The Basic Law mandated that key elements of the national welfare state would apply universally throughout the nation. At the same time, allowances were made within the Law for local governments to apply their own discretion in the way certain social services were administered.

From 1950 to 1969, West Germany experienced soaring economic growth that helped fund the massive expansion of its social welfare system. A highly complex civil service apparatus was responsible for managing and overseeing a vast array of public provisions. While sharing a commitment to democracy and a market economy with countries such as the United States, West Germany gave its government a much more prominent role in the country's economic affairs. While the market remained the principal mechanism by which most resources would be allocated in German society, the welfare state played a vital role in moderating many of the negative consequences associated with no-holds-barred free market competition. Under a 'historic compromise' between the political left and right, Germany's leaders adopted a 'social market economy'. Under this arrangement, the state assumed a formal role in facilitating business–labour wage compromises by providing workers with a variety of publicly funded social provisions. A number of social policy measures were achieved through the collective bargaining process. These included, for example, expanding social security provisions to greater numbers of citizens, increasing the amount of public housing available to working families, and adopting provisions for paid vacation time for employees. New legislation also mandated periodic adjustments to public pensions to reflect changes in wages and salaries.

In the 1950s, statutory health insurance was extended to larger groups of citizens, including students, farmers, and those with disabilities. By 1960, the total health expenditure, both public and private, accounted for 4.7 per cent of Germany's GDP. As health costs skyrocketed in the 1970s, however, the government felt compelled to enact a Health Cost Containment Law. The federal health finance and budget commission known as 'Concerted Action' (*Konzertierte Aktion*) was established to oversee a series of cost containment measures. Since it lacked sufficient political power to impose any serious cost containment measures, its activities proved to be largely symbolic.

Sweden

In the first three decades following the end of the Second World War, Sweden was applauded for sustaining one of the most comprehensive welfare systems in the capitalist world while simultaneously boasting high levels of productivity and economic growth. During the period from 1932 to 1976, a succession of centre-left Social Democratic governments consistently supported the expansion of social provisions. A broad political consensus was forged between those on the country's political right and left as they came together in support of common public policy agendas. Most notably, a historic compromise was reached between labour and business groups pertaining to areas such as workers' pensions, labour wages, and corporate taxes. As a result, Swedish workers enjoyed some of the most generous pensions offered anywhere in Europe, while the country's businesses and stockholders benefited from some of the lowest corporate tax rates in the industrialized world.

As Swedish industry expanded, and the economy flourished in the years following the Second World War, Social Democratic governments continued to support the expansion of the Swedish welfare state. Accordingly, Sweden's public sector bureaucracy and the administrative system increased in both size and scope. Inevitably, additional pressures were placed on public expenditures. Indeed, public sector spending as a share of GDP continued to grow steadily into the next decade. The 1955 National Insurance Law, for example, extended medical cash benefits (funded by sickness funds, taxes, and government subsidies) to all Swedish citizens. Public education, generous pension benefits, comprehensive healthcare, and social insurance for the unemployed were all extended under Sweden's state-supported collective bargaining system. These costly social provisions were funded largely through a combination of progressive taxes on workers' marginal incomes and direct employer contributions.

As the Swedish social welfare system continued to expand throughout the 1960s and 1970s, administrative costs continued to escalate. As a result, a heavy financial burden was placed on the country's taxpayers, with Swedish citizens becoming among the highest taxed in the capitalist world. Over time, Swedish voters predictably grew disenchanted with the government's financial management strategies and high taxes. In the general election of 1976, after nearly forty-four years in power, the Social Democrats finally faced defeat. The new conservative-leaning government was resolved to reduce the high costs associated with Sweden's welfare state, which had been developed under Social Democratic leadership over nearly half a century. However, conservative leaders found it politically untenable to deliver on their promises. The Social Democrats regained power in the election of 1979 and vowed to resume their commitment to the Swedish people. Having returned to power after only three years, Social Democrats enjoyed more than a decade of further uninterrupted rule. Throughout the 1980s, Swedes continued to enjoy high living standards and generous welfare benefits and services. More than 30 per cent of the workforce was employed in the public sector. Perhaps equally compelling is that nearly 60 per cent of the nation's GDP was spent on welfare provisions. Despite growing political pressures in the mid-1980s for the left-leaning government to rein in government expenditures in the face of increasing public-sector deficits and inflation, the Social Democrats made few adjustments. In fact, they managed to increase the child benefit allowance and extend unemployment benefits. While they were ultimately forced to accept modest cost-containment measures in the base amounts used to calculate certain social benefits, the Swedish welfare state remained largely intact from 1982 to 1991.

The United States

The days immediately following the stock market crash of 1929 proved to be among the darkest in American history. The nation's financial markets plummeted and millions became unemployed. The election of FDR in 1932 and the introduction of the New Deal reshaped American social welfare policy on a historic scale. In his first hundred days in office, the fiscally minded president introduced a series of modest policies aimed at ameliorating the effects of the crisis. Over the next eight years, however, his administration adopted a more ambitious and aggressive set of government-led initiatives aimed at stabilizing the country's economy. In an effort to create new jobs and provide new sources of hydroelectric power to boost the economy, FDR worked with Congress to approve funding for the Tennessee Valley Authority (TVA). Established in 1933, this federally owned corporation became the nation's first regional planning agency. Employing countless engineers, civil planners, and workers, the TVA oversaw the construction and management of massive infrastructural projects, including dams and waterways that were aimed at promoting new development in agricultural areas. At the same time, agricultural subsidies were introduced to help boost commodity prices, which had fallen during the crash of 1929.

With the passage of the National Industrial Recovery Act in 1935, workers were empowered with a new set of collective bargaining rights, which allowed them to organize for higher wages, new benefits, and improved working conditions. Most importantly, however, the Act established a new federally supported Public Works Administration. Unprecedented in scale and scope, this became an important part of FDR's comprehensive government-led 'demand management' programme to revive the economy. Nearly $6 billion was allocated to fund large-scale public works programmes including the construction of new highways, waterways, bridges, hospitals, and educational facilities. Most of the funding was issued through contracts with private firms, in order to support private business growth, create new employment, and bolster the purchasing power of consumers.

During the same period, FDR established the Works Progress Administration (WPA) as part of his grand vision for the country's economic recovery. Perhaps the best-known of the New Deal programmes, the WPA ultimately provided a variety of employment opportunities to those who would have otherwise been marginalized. Most of the WPA workforce consisted of unskilled labourers who were employed to work on small-scale construction and improvement projects. Under the leadership and supervision of social worker Harry Hopkins, millions of jobs were created, covering a myriad of projects related to public roads, government buildings, parks and recreation, as well as reforestation. Many Americans, however, were relegated to performing menial and unessential jobs and tasks. Additionally, the government commissioned thousands of murals and sculptures which adorned public buildings across the country. Additional funds were earmarked for the theatrical and performing arts. The WPA was later placed under the Federal Works Agency as part of the 1939 Reorganization Act, before being completely phased out in 1943.

The establishment of America's entitlement system became the crowning achievement of the New Deal. In 1935, FDR signed the Social Security Act, which provided public pension support to millions of retired Americans and also established the country's first national unemployment insurance scheme. The Social Security Act was designed not only to prevent suffering but also to alleviate it. The programme's designers sought to improve the lives of those already living in poverty through the introduction of government transfer payments to those in dire need of relief. Much of the funding associated with relief programmes for the poor was provided through the 1935 Aid to Dependent Children Act, which established the programme later known as Aid to Families with Dependent Children (AFDC).

The New Deal policies and programmes fuelled the expansion of the American federal government. It soon became apparent that the executive branch would need to be restructured to successfully implement many of its policies and mandates. A select committee on Administrative Management, popularly known as the Brownlow Committee, was established to create a more tightly structured and coherently managed administrative apparatus. A leading public administration scholar (and former New York City official) by the name of Luther Gulick was invited by FDR to help organize this comprehensive effort. FDR sought Gulick's counsel when developing strategies for improving the function and operation of America's public administration system.

In 1937 Gulick and his well-known British colleague, Lyndall Urwick, published 'Papers on the Science of Administration' related to Gulick's work on the Brownlow Committee. Building upon Frederick Taylor's scientific principles and methods emphasizing 'the one best way' approach, as well as Henri Fayol's functional analysis of administrative management, Gulick and Urwick introduced seven essential functions of management. Presented under the acronym POSDCORB, these essential functions consisted of Planning, Organizing, Staffing, Directing,

Coordinating, Reporting, and Budgeting. The characteristics of POSDCORB as discussed by Gulick and Urwick are as follows: '*Planning*, that is working out in broad outline the things that need to be done and the methods for doing them to accomplish the purpose set for the enterprise; *Organizing*, that is the establishment of the formal structure of authority through which work subdivisions are arranged, defined, and coordinated for the defined objective; *Staffing*, that is the personnel function of bringing in and training the staff and maintaining favorable conditions of work; *Directing*, that is the continuous task of making decisions and embodying them in specific and general orders and instructions and serving as the leader of the enterprise; *Coordinating*, that is the all-important duty of interrelating the various parts of the work; *Reporting*, that is keeping those to whom the executive is responsible informed as to what is going on, which includes keeping both the executive and subordinates informed through records, research, and inspection; *Budgeting*, with all that goes with budgeting in the form of planning, accounting and control.'

America's entrance into the Second World War created millions of employment opportunities. In the years following the war, with its industrial base intact, America led the world in industrial productivity. As the American economy flourished throughout the 1950s, unemployment became less of a political concern. By the 1960s, however, mounting public concerns over America's unequal distribution of wealth (particularly in parts of the rural South and urban North) inspired the nation's progressive politicians to return to the issue of poverty alleviation. A number of landmark public sector programmes were adopted under the Democratic presidential administrations of John F. Kennedy and Lyndon B. Johnson, aimed at assisting America's working and indigent poor. The Johnson administration's 'Great Society' and 'War on Poverty' programmes became the centrepieces of this effort. A major entitlement programme, Medicare, was introduced, guaranteeing health coverage to those 65 years of age and older. Medicaid was

Box 4 Clash of the intellectual titans

In 1952, the *American Political Science Review* featured an article that would ignite a fiery discussion between Dwight Waldo and Herbert Simon, then two of the leading heavyweights in the field of public administration. The much discussed Waldo–Simon dispute helped crystallize the growing polemic in the field between fact-based, 'hard science'-oriented approaches, stressing 'what is the case?', and normative lines of inquiry emphasizing 'what is to be done?' In the *APSR* article, entitled *Development of Theory of Democratic Administration*, Waldo emphasized the 'limitations of science' by sharply challenging the reigning belief in 'efficiency as the central concept in our science'. Waldo insisted that 'efficiency' should not be treated as a universal axiom, but rather as a contested value that must be explored and debated on philosophical grounds. Indeed, Waldo believed that 'the established techniques of science are inapplicable to studying' the things he considered to be the essential elements of public administration—'thinking' and 'valuing human beings'. 'Questions of value', Waldo reasoned, 'were not amenable to scientific treatment.' Contrastingly, Simon sought to emphasize an empirical, science-based approach to both administrative analysis and decision-making. In so doing, he asserted that logical-positivist-driven administrative 'science' should take precedence over value-based approaches. Through his writings on *Administrative Behavior*, Simon would distinguish himself as an organizational theorist as opposed to a pure public administration scholar. Indeed, he would later be heralded as one of the leading figures of modern (scientific-based) organizational theory both within the field of public administration and beyond.

unveiled soon after, extending basic health coverage to poor American families. Over the next few years, additional federal programmes were introduced, ranging from housing subsidies and school lunch programmes to family planning and women's support services. The federal government attempted to break the cycle of poverty by extending additional public services to children and their parents. The 1964 Equal Opportunity Act, for example, provided federal financial support for educational and job training programmes, as well as creating new sources of funding for early age educational programmes such as Head Start.

During the late 1960s and early 1970s, the costs associated with many of these social programmes began outpacing existing financial means. The government ran large deficits, and it increased taxes. The conservative leadership of President Richard Nixon attacked Johnson's War on Poverty as a source of uncontrollable government spending. Moreover, conservative economists such as Milton Friedman and Herbert Stein convinced the Nixon administration that many of the social programmes adopted during the Johnson era helped support a culture of welfare dependency.

The 1970s proved to be a tumultuous time in American history. During this period, America faced rising unemployment, high inflation, and declining economic productivity. Attempts to bolster economic output through increased public spending on public programmes (consistent with Keynesian demand-management strategies) only seemed to make things worse. As a result, welfare expenditures were viewed as a luxury that the government and the middle class could no longer afford to support.

Britain

The founding principles underpinning the modern British welfare state were outlined in *The Beveridge Report* released in 1942. Officially known as the Social Insurance and Allied Services Report, it would serve as a general 'main blue print' of the 1945–51 Labour government's historic welfare state initiative. It has been suggested that the economic details contained within this historic document were designed in consultation with John Maynard Keynes. This helped boost the document's credibility in the eyes of influential politicians in parliament. Moreover, the report cemented the British government's guarantee of a 'national minimum standard' of economic security to its individual citizens. While insisting that basic economic security was a political right conferred by citizenship, Lord Beveridge simultaneously expressed concerns over the potential for free rider abuse and the propensity for creating a culture of 'welfare dependency'. He insisted, therefore, that reciprocal responsibilities be placed on citizens to provide for themselves whenever possible.

Beveridge believed that government not only had the responsibility, but also the ability, to eliminate poverty by providing basic levels of public support to those whose livelihood and earning power was disrupted by structural economic changes and crises. Toward those ends, *The Beveridge Report* addressed five 'giant evils' that he claimed 'no democracy can afford for its citizens' in modern society: 'want, disease, ignorance, squalor, and idleness'. Beveridge argued that these five ills represented a threat to the overall well-being of British society. He insisted that they must be eradicated in order for democratic society to continue to thrive. Beveridge asserted, however, that government needed to adopt the proper means for addressing these social ills in a manner that would not obstruct or stifle personal initiative—nor encourage welfare dependency. Many of Beveridge's ideas (though not all) helped shape the values and goals underlying the modern British welfare state. While some claim that Beveridge's direct involvement in most programmatic details was rather limited, the influence of his core principles in guiding the direction of policymakers is difficult to dispute.

In the years following the Second World War, the government adopted a universal social insurance scheme covering all British citizens. Under its comprehensive framework, workers made individual contributions from their weekly paychecks in exchange for a wide range of social provisions. These included universal health and medical coverage, unemployment insurance, senior pensions, maternity support, workplace injury insurance, and burial cost supplements. Of the five evils named in the report only the condition of 'want' was addressed directly. That said, the report helped lay the foundation for the passage of subsequent legislation covering the remaining evils of 'disease, ignorance, squalor, and idleness'. Moreover, the report extended the political definition of 'liberty' from 'freedom to speak, write, and vote' to 'freedom from want, disease, ignorance, squalor, and idleness'. Perhaps most importantly, *The Beveridge Report* directed people's attention towards the importance of adopting a comprehensive welfare system (Box 5).

In the 1970s the British government confronted a combination of international financial shocks, high inflation, and increasing levels of unemployment. The Labour government initially responded with state-led demand-management strategies, which ultimately proved ineffective. In 1976, Britain's economy deteriorated to the point where an International Monetary Fund (IMF) bailout was required to keep the country's currency from completely collapsing. In the months that followed, public officials and citizens alike began raising serious questions about the affordability of maintaining the current welfare state and, more generally,

---

Box 5 Main legislative measures inspired by *The Beveridge Report*

1945 Family Allowances Act
1946 National Insurance Act
1946 National Insurance (Industrial Injuries) Act
1946 National Health Service Act (implemented July 1948)
1947 Town and Country Planning Act
1947 New Towns Act
1948 National Assistance Act
1948 Children Act
1949 Housing Act

Table 2 Government employment, 1870–1980 (as percentage of total employment in selected nations)

Nation	1870	1913	1937	1960	1980
Germany	1.2	2.4	4.3	9.9	14.6
Sweden	2.2	3.5	4.7	12.8	30.3
Great Britain	4.9	4.1	6.5	14.8	21.1
United States	2.9	3.7	6.8	14.7	15.1

Sources: OECD (2015), 'Employment in the public sector', Government at a Glance 2000–2015, OECD Publishing, Paris. DOI: http://dx.doi.org/10.1787/gov_glance-2015-22-en; adapted from Messaoud Hammouya, 'Statistics on public sector employment: methodology, structures and trends' (Bureau of Statistics International Labour Office, Geneva, 1999) © ILO, 1999.

about the proper role and function of government in the economy. When Margaret Thatcher assumed power in 1979, she noted that in nearly 70 per cent of British households, at least one family member received some form of cash welfare benefit. Determined to roll back state expenditures for social welfare spending, Thatcher's Conservative government waged a concerted assault on the country's public sector. We will examine this more closely in Chapter 5.

The administrative systems that developed in the late 1800s were inadequate to address many of the complex political and public problems of the industrialized world. The evolution of the modern welfare state reflects the dynamic nature of contemporary society. As societies have become more democratic, citizens have placed increasing demands on government to provide more public services (Table 2). In order to meet the growing demands and expectations of an increasingly complex society, government bureaucracies and public administration systems have been compelled to expand. In the 1980s, conservative-leaning political movements in both right-of-centre and left-of-centre political parties began mobilizing against 'big government' and its twin redistributive engines—high taxes and large deficits.

Chapter 5
The New Public Management goes global

The so called 'golden age' of the Keynesian State was turbulently interrupted by a series of economic shocks in the 1970s. An oil embargo led by OPEC (the Organization of Petroleum Exporting Countries) caused the world price of crude oil to soar. A combination of high inflation and rising unemployment ('stagflation') immediately ensued. Corporate profits quickly evaporated and stock prices plummeted. Meanwhile, many governments in the industrialized countries of the world stood by helplessly. Confronted with mass unemployment and intense social despair, some 'enterprising' leaders saw great potential for growth in the financial services sector. Fuelled by new government initiatives aimed at deregulating financial markets and aided by technological breakthroughs in electronic trading and financial instruments, a new era of global financial-based capitalism (known as 'financialization') was born. Now free to move billions of dollars across the globe instantaneously, savvy investors wagered their fortunes in countries whose policies could ensure the highest returns in the shortest amount of time. As a result, modern governments were under intense pressure to 'rationalize' their tax systems and cut public spending in order to demonstrate their 'investment-worthiness'. In this process many public goods would be eviscerated in order to attract a new breed of voracious global investors.

Traditional administrative hierarchies were regarded as too rigid and inflexible to adapt to the dynamic political and economic forces that were unleashed in the global age. Senior level public administrators and public leaders across the world increasingly looked toward a new set of market-oriented strategies in the hope of bolstering bureaucracy efficiency and maximizing taxpayer dollars. Emphasizing private sector values such as 'timeliness', 'responsiveness', and 'cost savings', a new kind of 'managerialism', that would later become known as the New Public Management (NPM), began to take root in some of the world's leading public bureaucracies (Box 6).

Box 6 New Public Administration

Though sharing a similar acronym with the NPM, the New Public Administration (NPA) was a very different kind of management paradigm that emerged during the 1960s. Placing 'public service' at the heart of its managerial credo, the NPA adopted a set of management principles that emphasized values of 'civic virtue' and 'citizen empowerment'. Associated with the pioneering work of Abraham Maslow and his colleagues in the school of 'humanistic psychology', NPA advocates believed that creating organizational conditions that contributed to the emotional and physical well-being of its employees was essential to administrative productivity. In the late 1960s, NPA scholar Dwight Waldo hosted a historic conference aimed at fostering a fresh and new dialogue governing the 'future' of public administration. In an effort to explore innovative approaches, Waldo invited a number of budding pioneers in the field to participate. Railing against 'racial discrimination', 'social injustice', and 'inequality', the young and energetic attendees sought to reorient the field of public administration, away from the 'narrow' pursuit of administrative efficiency and towards 'democratic equality' and 'social justice'. The NPA, however,

> was not without its critics. A number of prominent figures in the mainstream academy of public administration voiced concerns that it was replacing 'scientifically-testable' management principles with 'soft' knowledge that stemmed from idealistic sentiments.

In a 2001 article entitled 'Public management reform and economic and social development' in the *OECD Budget Journal*, former Australian finance minister Michael Keating summarized the forces behind the NPM reforms that had been attempted over the previous decade and a half in his country. These included: '1) the level of taxation, the budget deficit and/or public debt was too high, and could become even worse if no action were taken; 2) government programmes too often failed to achieve their objectives and/or were not cost effective so that they did not represent value for money; 3) the administrative machinery was not sufficiently responsive to the needs of clients including ministers themselves; and 4) government itself was part of the problem, having become too big and too intrusive.' While differing definitions and explanations have surfaced over the years, noted public administration scholar Donald Kettl has outlined six core characteristics that appear to be shared in the vast majority of literature related to the NPM: 'productivity, marketization, service orientation, decentralization, a policy orientation, and accountability for results'.

The first wave of NPM approaches surfaced in the political reform agendas under the conservative governments of England's Margaret Thatcher (1979–90), America's Ronald Reagan (1981–9), Australia's Malcolm Fraser (1975–83), and Canada's Brian Mulroney (1984–93). While prime minister Margaret Thatcher's government was one of the first to formally adopt NPM-based approaches in the late 1970s, a number of related principles

> **Box 7 Neoliberalism**
>
> The NPM is a governance paradigm that is sympathetic with a set of market-oriented principles that are rooted in a political-economic doctrine known as 'Neoliberalism'. Neoliberalism was first coined by a group of politically moderate economists and legal scholars affiliated with the 'Freiburg School' which emerged during the post-World War I period in Germany. The term was later used as a catchphrase to refer to a 'return to the market' campaign led by economists such as Nobel prize winners Milton Friedman and Friedrich von Hayek. Glorifying the virtues of individual self-interest, economic efficiency, and unbridled competition, neoliberalism became associated with welfare state retrenchment and economic austerity. In the 1970s, a more extreme strand of this doctrine, known as neoliberalismo, was adopted by oppressive dictators in Latin America, such as Chilean President Augusto Pinochet, as part of their stringent antisocialist campaigns. In the 1990s, however, the term was employed by leftist academics in their scathing critiques of the United States' policy initiatives aimed at spreading American-style 'cowboy capitalism' to the former Soviet bloc countries in Eastern Europe following the collapse of communism. Over the last three decades, neoliberal-based NPM programmes, emphasizing private sector efficiency measures and performance standards, have been undertaken by different political figures. Some of the best-known include: America's Ronald Reagan and Bill Clinton; Britain's Margaret Thatcher and Tony Blair; Canada's Brian Mulroney; Australia's Malcolm Fraser, Robert Hawke, and Paul Keating.

were quickly adopted by governments across the globe operating at all levels. Some of the earliest NPM applications were observed in the municipal areas of Northern California where enduring recessionary conditions forced city leaders to find innovative ways to cut government expenditures. Governments

in New Zealand and Australia would quickly follow with
NPM-based administrative agendas of their own. Before long, by
the mid-1980s, a majority of OECD countries would introduce
NPM administrative practices into their public sector
organizations as well.

Grounded in an emergent doctrine known as 'neoliberalism', the
NPM venerates the self-regulating free market as a virtuous
model for civil governance (Box 7). Accordingly, the NPM
subordinates principles and processes associated with traditional
public administration focused on 'equity' and 'fairness' to
business-oriented principles which emphasize efficiency standards
and productivity targets. This shift towards private sector
'managerialism' has compelled public sector agencies to apply
(or in many cases misapply) principles from specifications-based
stratagems such as total quality management (TQM), 'Lean Six
Sigma', and 'Management by Objectives'. Under the managerialist
logic, 'public servants' were converted into public sector 'service
providers' whose purposes had been reoriented around satisfying
customers' needs.

The first NPM wave

Upon taking the oath of office in 1981, President Ronald Reagan
revealed his new Program for Economic Recovery. The president's
controversial programme, which reduced the tax burden on
America's highest income earners, would become the cornerstone
of his economic agenda known as 'Reaganomics'. Comprising
part of a wider ideological assault on the public sector,
'Reaganomics' included substantial cuts in a wide array of
government social welfare programmes. In his pursuit of smaller,
and hence less 'obstructive', government, Reagan adopted a host of
NPM-inspired 'devolutionary' reform measures aimed at transferring
federal regulatory power to state and local administrative units.
Under this initiative, known as 'New Federalism', many new

administrative responsibilities would now be carried out by the states—often with little financial assistance from the national government.

Reagan relied on the use of a budgetary instrument known as 'block grants' in a strategic effort to transfer both fiscal responsibility and the management of many social programmes, ranging from school lunch programmes to Medicaid, to the states. While major entitlement programmes, such as Social Security, would continue to be managed and overseen by the federal government, the conservative president sought to introduce a lean voucher system into the country's Medicare system in an effort to encourage 'competition' and 'efficiency'. While ultimately unsuccessful, Reagan's efforts represented an unprecedented move to introduce private sector principles to the administrative process involved in delivering a major social services entitlement programme.

Reagan's New Federalist agenda was deeply embedded in an ideological commitment to reducing the size of government. This was a doctrine also preached by the 'Public Choice' school of economics. Asserting that individual citizens 'vote with their feet', members of this school argued that local governments were more in touch with the needs of their 'clients'. Additionally, they argued, decentralized, slimmed-down forms of administrative governance were less likely to 'obstruct' private sector productivity through 'unneeded' regulations. In seeking to protect individual choice and private initiative as the highest social priority, the public choice school insisted that rigorous 'economic' principles and tools be used to assess the 'worthiness' of spending 'hard earned' taxpayers' dollars on specific social programmes.

'Reaganomics' was heavily influenced by the work of William A. Niskanen, one of the president's leading economic advisers. A student of the Nobel prize-winning economist Milton Friedman, Niskanen's enormously influential 1971 work on *Bureaucracy and*

Representative Government served to inspire NPM movements across the globe. Niskanen argued that 'rational' public sector bureaucrats and legislative leaders will seek ways to expand their own scope and power at the expense of the taxpayers and social efficiency. Niskanen asserted that politicians tend to overspend on politically popular programmes in an effort to win more votes; public administrators, who are charged with implementing these same programmes, are always looking for ways to increase the size and scope of their government bureaucracies. Niskanen concluded logically that even in circumstances where public officials might be able to find ways to perform their duties and carry out their functions with fewer economic resources, they have little incentive to do so. On the contrary, public administrators will always seek to 'maximize' the budgets that have been allocated to them by politically minded legislators.

Impressed by Niskanen's argument, President Reagan signed Executive Order 12291, which required that public agencies use cost-benefit analysis to evaluate all proposals involving regulatory and social spending. Under its use, the budgets of many social programmes and public agencies responsible for administrative oversight and enforcement were either cut substantially or eliminated completely. Indeed, the regulatory powers wielded by government organizations like the Environmental Protection Agency (EPA) were significantly curtailed using these methods.

While British prime minister Margaret Thatcher shared Reagan's contempt for 'big government', she exhibited little sympathy for his New Federalism's emphasis on decentralization and empowerment of local government. Indeed, Thatcher viewed local public administrators as highly inefficient and susceptible to political corruption. Accordingly, Thatcher sought to replace traditional local tax rates with a new 'poll tax'—or 'community charge'—in an effort to severely restrict revenues available to local councils. Under heavy political fire, the prime minister would later reverse this unpopular decision.

Detesting the growth of government, which she associated with 'uncontrollable' rates of public spending, Thatcher strongly condemned the practice of taxing private wealth to finance 'inefficient' government-administered programmes and policies. At the heart of Thatcher's public sector retrenchment campaign was her controversial 'Medium Term Financial Strategy' (MTFS). The MTFS would redirect the focus of Britain's treasury and spending ministers away from a short-term tax-and-spend scheme toward a longer term strategic initiative aimed at limiting her country's monetary growth. The strict spending limits mandated by the MTFS naturally imposed new challenges on public policymakers and public administrators. In order to justify her position, the provocative prime minister went to great lengths to convince her peers of the merits of her austere NPM-based public sector retrenchment campaign for the 'greater good' of society. To help her make her case for retrenchment, Thatcher made Niskanen's book on *Bureaucracy* 'required reading' for all members of her senior cabinet. Supported by a fiery band of party loyalists in parliament (known as Thatcherites), the ultra-conservative leader continued on a vigorous crusade to institute a rich mix of NPM-based reforms which included significantly reducing government regulations, and privatizing national industries.

Thatcher believed that the management and leadership structure reigning over Britain's enormous civil service bureaucracy had become inert and inflexible. In order to jump-start the implementation of her revolutionary NPM-based efficiency and service reforms, Thatcher adopted a comprehensive administrative programme requiring public 'managers' to assume responsibility for 'managing' their organizations more effectively. Under a neoliberal programme known as 'Next Steps', various public services would be delivered through market-like arrangements and overseen by managers who possessed the administrative authority and resources required to fulfil their mandates. Specific service delivery tasks and functions that had previously been carried out by the various government departments would now be reassigned to independently run single-function-oriented agencies and organizations. Under this innovative administrative framework, ministers remained in charge of creating public policy, while the management functions and responsibilities associated with implementation were administered through independent agencies. Now operating under strict 'private-sector-like' accountability standards, the performance levels of agency managers were closely monitored by their related ministerial department heads.

As part of her broader NPM agenda, Thatcher oversaw the sale of a substantial number of state-owned industries to private firms and investors. Her well-known privatization drive began in the early 1980s with the sale of such recognizable industry giants as British Aerospace, British Rail, and Associated British Ports, and later continued with the privatization of Rolls-Royce Aircraft Engines and British Petroleum among others. In many cases, state-run enterprises were sold below market values. This was done, in part, under the assumption that their new managers would use the surplus funds to modernize plant facilities to make them globally competitive. Margaret Thatcher's successor, John Major, would later go on to privatize some of the 'Next Steps' agencies as well as expand the practice of contracting out various other public services.

Believing that local council administrators had grossly mismanaged the construction and management of Britain's public housing sector, the Thatcher government arranged the private sale of large amounts of government-owned properties. Previously, these councils had retained administrative control over millions of properties completely untethered from essential legal guidelines or procedural accountability. In order to promote increased administrative efficiency in housing management, the prime minister enacted the Housing Act of 1980. Under this initiative, long-term tenants with financial means were provided with a 'right to buy' option and significant legal provisions were adopted to ensure the property rights of these tenant 'customers'. Unfortunately, Thatcher's well-meaning 'reforms' were poorly executed. In the absence of any comprehensive publicly subsidized financing scheme, many tenants could not afford to purchase their newly 'privatized' homes. As a result, they were forced to move to cheaper and often less desirable neighbourhoods, thereby exacerbating existing disparities among Britain's social classes.

Similarly, when faced with massive structural unemployment resulting from Britain's waning industrial sector, Thatcher put her unwavering trust in the hands of the 'free market' to determine which occupations would be protected or abolished. Believing that Britain's economic future rested in the hands of the financial services sector, her government adopted a series of policies that helped accelerate the rebirth of the 'City' of London as a leading global trading centre. As part of this 'transformation' the prime minister imposed strict NPM-based private-sector performance standards on public-sector-controlled coal pits, mines, and manufacturing plants. Remaining faithful to the principles of the NPM, Thatcher mandated that goals and objectives were to be clearly outlined and outputs evaluated according to strict efficiency standards.

Driven by her fervent desire to cut state expenditures, Thatcher zeroed-in on inefficiencies associated with Britain's state welfare sector. Among the most spectacular and controversial was her high-profile crusade to reform child benefit assistance that had been made available universally to all working mothers irrespective of their income and means. Insisting that social security and child benefit programmes should be accessible only to the 'truly needy', Thatcher sought to impose strict means tests in order to reduce the financial burden on the country's taxpayers. The prime minister, though famous for her uncompromising spirit, was forced to scale back these reforms in the face of a severe political backlash from voters and even some members of her own party.

Undeterred, the 'Iron Lady' pressed ahead with efforts to reform Britain's 'antiquated' public pension system. Thatcher sought to 'liberate' employee accounts from the control of the unions by allowing individual workers to carry their investitures with them when they moved from one job to the next. The evisceration of rigid state-imposed hurdles that tied employees' pensions to their existing employers, Thatcher argued, would help encourage employees to seek higher skilled and higher paying positions. Confronted once more with strong political resistance from a hostile political electorate, Thatcher was forced to moderate her reform ambitions. The resolute prime minister was, however, ultimately successful in implementing a number of NPM-style administrative improvements to existing means-testing eligibility requirements. In the end, her government was able to make considerable strides towards streamlining rules and procedures in ways that promoted greater consistency and equity in the distribution of benefits.

Asserting that the root cause of all of the problems associated with Britain's National Health Service (NHS) was structurally embedded in bureaucratic inefficiency rather than a lack of proper funding, Thatcher looked to the free market for innovative solutions. Unshaken in her faith in NPM-based remedies, the prime minister mandated that public hospitals field bids from private healthcare providers. In that vein, the Thatcher government instituted 'flexibilist' reform legislation that provided local health authorities with greater administrative power and authority to help manage rising healthcare costs by contracting out to the private sector for the delivery of many public health services. When opposition arose within her own Conservative party to her austere economic reforms and neoliberal-based NPM programmes, Thatcher defiantly proclaimed, 'You turn if you want to. The lady's not for turning'.

Australia

Australia's experiments with NPM-inspired 'managerialist' ideas and practices were not dissimilar to those adopted by its

American and British counterparts. Indeed, it is a documented fact that Australian Public Service (APS) officers and administrators were heavily inspired by the NPM experiments undertaken by the Thatcher and Reagan governments. As the public administration wing of the Australian federal government, the APS's NPM-based public sector reforms unfolded in three discrete stages. Initially introduced to the public by the left-leaning Australian Labour Party Governments (ALPG) of prime ministers Robert Hawke in 1983 and Paul Keating in 1996, the NPM programme would later be adopted more strictly by the conservative Liberal-National Party Coalition Government (LNPCG) of prime minister John Howard.

Times were tough for Australians in the early 1980s. The Keynesian administrative framework governing fiscal management proved unable to provide Australian leaders with satisfactory solutions to their country's deepening economic crisis. As a former trade union leader, prime minister Hawke was under intense political pressure to provide relief and assurance to his workers. Under the leadership of Hawke's treasury minister, Paul Keating, a select cadre of technically skilled civil administrators, known as mandarins, were solicited to help craft a neoliberal macroeconomic policy package. Among its important features were the introduction of a business-friendly tax system and a series of public spending cuts in an effort to tackle inflation and government debt. The pragmatic prime minister also reached across ideological lines to both labour unions and private businesses, asking for help in implementing a host of key NPM reforms to address steadily declining rates of productivity in the country's distressed industrial sector. Additionally, this reform initiative would feature a bold deregulation and privatization drive that would contribute to dramatic changes to the country's 'Government Business Enterprise' (GBE) sector.

In the mid-1980s a new framework was introduced by the Financial Management Improvement Programme (FMIP), which 'institutionalized' key components of the NPM in Australia's public sector. Designed to address 'gross' systemic inefficiencies embedded in the procedural operations across a number of APS agencies, the FMIP was a comprehensive strategic management programme that adopted 'results-based' principles to improve organizational performance. Under these provisions, public managers were now 'incentivized' to adopt new measures that would streamline operational process in areas ranging from organizational planning and budget forecasting all the way to programme implementation and evaluation.

A number of APS reforms were specifically aimed at improving the administrative coordination between national and state governments. As part of this effort, greater administrative discretion and accountability involved with implementation was devolved to subnational authorities. A number of high profile NPM initiatives were undertaken in areas ranging from financial and human resource management to privatization of the GBEs. Once in power, Keating adopted a comprehensive NPM programme aimed at restructuring his country's antiquated regulatory policies governing GBEs so that they could compete globally. Contributing more than 10 per cent to the nation's GDP, GBEs play a significant role in Australia's economy. Public utilities, for example, such as rail, electricity, gas, and water, collectively represent nearly 5 per cent of the country's productive wealth. Equally impressive is that GBEs, as a whole, contribute almost 40 per cent to the country's private business sector stock. Providing essential services ranging from telecommunications to hydroelectric power, some of Australia's leading GBEs include such well-known service giants as Telstra Telecom and Snowy Mountains Hydroelectric Authority. Keating adopted private sector customer service methods, such as 'commercialization', in order to improve service delivery. The next level in the NPM reform process was known as 'corporatization', in which government authorities gradually relinquished operational control of certain GBEs to private managers. The final phase of the NPM evolution involved 'privatization', in which GBEs were sold into private hands. Well-known examples include international corporate brands such as Qantas Airlines and Commonwealth Bank.

The NPM reforms that were attempted by the various Australian governments did not sufficiently address deep structural problems that had long been engrained in Australia's public sector. Critics charged that the APS's FMIP reform framework did not go far enough and amounted to little more than a 'repository for a series of unconnected management ideas' and processes. The APS system needed to be completely overhauled in ways that would genuinely integrate the disparate managerial functions at both the federal and subnational levels in order to improve inter-agency coordination.

The second NPM wave

A 'second wave' of the NPM was most notably associated with the policy agendas of America's Bill Clinton and Britain's Tony Blair. Their neoliberal agendas adopted many of the same principles of the Reagan and Thatcher period but included several social justice based initiatives including comprehensive welfare-to-work reform strategies, new minimum wage policies, and the expansion of tax relief schemes for the working poor and their families.

Immediately upon assuming power in January 1993, American president Bill Clinton announced his administration's firm commitment to fiscal stability. Ever conscious of the pressures that uncontrolled public spending could place on rising inflation, the new president outlined definitive budgetary limits on government department expenditures. To meet these targets, the Clinton administration sought new ways of creating a 'leaner' and more efficient public sector. As a result, the moderate-left president adopted an NPM agenda known as 'Reinventing Government'. The leading proponents of this approach, Ted Gaebler and David Osborne, sought to promote a new kind of 'catalytic government', in which public officials should 'steer' policy agendas, but a variety of public and private agencies would be involved in the actual 'rowing', or day-to-day implementation and delivery of public services and programmes. Gaebler and Osborne's ten principles of 'catalytic government' emphasized a competitive, results-oriented, public administration system.

The Clinton administration's National Partnership for Reinventing Government included the implementation of National Performance Reviews, which were employed to reduce government waste and promote administrative efficiency and ensure greater bureaucratic accountability. In much the same way, the Blair government adopted Comprehensive Spending Reviews as well as Public Service Agreements to promote greater coordination among the Treasury and various spending departments of the cabinet in an effort to find the most efficient use of resources. In addition, both governments adopted comprehensive budget strategies that outlined long-term spending targets.

Successful implementation of the second wave of NPM policies would require heavy levels of coordination and interaction among various agencies and actors operating within the discrete levels of government and the private business sector. Unfortunately, many of these complexities were often not accounted for in the design and implementation of these policy strategies, resulting in management nightmares (Box 8).

In an attempt to address concerns that 'antiquated regulatory policies' were obstructing entrepreneurial initiatives, Clinton implemented a number of deregulation measures in order to provide the financial services sector with increased flexibility and autonomy so that they were free to take advantage of new financial opportunities emerging in the global marketplace. These included, for example, dismantling many of the legal walls separating the practices of commercial and investment banking organizations as well as those dividing insurance and securities firms. The devastating risks associated with such deregulation

> **Box 8 Neoliberalism as NPM: ten government objectives**
>
> 1. Catalytic government: steering rather than rowing
> 2. Community-owned government: empowering rather than serving
> 3. Competitive government: injecting competition into service
> 4. Mission-driven government: transforming rule-driven organizations
> 5. Results-oriented government: funding outcomes, not inputs
> 6. Customer-driven government: meeting the needs of the customer, not the bureaucracy
> 7. Enterprising government: earning rather than spending
> 8. Anticipatory government: prevention rather than cure
> 9. Decentralized government: from hierarchy to participation and teamwork
> 10. Market-oriented government: leveraging change through the market
>
> *Source*: David Osborne and Ted Gaebler, 'Reinventing government (1992)', cited in Robert B. Denhardt, *Theories of Public Organization*, 5th ed., pp. 145–6.

measures, however, would not be fully realized until the catastrophic collapse of the world's financial and real estate markets in 2008–9.

In order to address structural unemployment and financial hardships caused by the transformation from the 'old' manufacturing-based economy to the 'new financial-based economy', Clinton sought out NPM strategies to promote a modern, highly skilled, flexible workforce. Clinton's brand of 'workfare' was meant to innovatively combine labour skill development training with public assistance for the unemployed, without subjecting them to 'welfare dependency'. It has been documented that Clinton's 'welfare-to-work' programme was inspired, in part, by Ronald Reagan's Family Support Act of 1988. Clinton cultivated political support for his agenda from a growing neoliberal movement within his own party that were labelled 'New Democrats'. Comprised of a new breed of moderate-left politicians, such as Al Gore, Dave McCurdy, Ed Kilgore, and Joseph Lieberman, this motley group shared Clinton's desire to combine their party's traditional commitment to 'collective welfare' with NPM principles of 'individual responsibility' and 'accountability'. As part of a broader NPM programme, President Clinton supported the 1996 Welfare Reform Act, which replaced the Aid to Dependent Children programme that had been established by FDR back in the 1930s. The Clinton administration's 'reinventing-government'-led programme of 'workfare' now mandated 'work' in exchange for receiving welfare benefits. Under its strict provisions, recipients could only draw assistance for a maximum of two years before they were required to obtain gainful employment or enrol in new job training programmes. After five years of cumulative assistance a recipient's benefits would be terminated. The policy allowed public administrators to make special provisions for childcare and medical insurance to support short-term unemployed mothers. Tough mandates limiting the duration of welfare payments, however, made it difficult for single mothers to enrol in the necessary schooling required for them to qualify for better paying jobs.

Under Clinton's 'reinventing government' initiative, much like the Reagan administration's NPM programme, numerous social services administered by county and municipal authorities were contracted out to private sector companies. In many cases this stymied the delivery of essential support services such as childcare assistance for single-income mothers. In these instances, complex coordination between public administrative authorities and private entities required to successfully implement many of these policies and programmes was often wanting. We will explore some of the major implementation issues involved with intergovernmental relations in Chapter 6.

Determined to create an economy of only 'haves and have yachts', the left-of-centre governments led by prime minister Tony Blair and later Gordon Brown would adopt some of the most spectacular and politically popular neoliberal programmes of all time. To accomplish his vision of this 'new Britain', Blair understood that he would have to court new groups of global investors. This would involve changing the way Britain's public sector 'did business'. Having learned from the failures of his predecessors, Blair instituted important NPM reforms through heavy coordination with the Treasury (and other spending departments), cabinet committees, task forces, business groups, and many others. As part of this effort, over 300 task forces were created to advise and support ministers in order to facilitate cooperation among central government departments. Consistent with NPM prescriptions, the Treasury began publishing a pre-budget report or 'green budget' in order to promote greater transparency and accountability. Additionally, the deficit-conscious prime minister and his cabinet introduced a Code for Fiscal Stability which emphasized five tenets of sound fiscal management: 'transparency', 'stability', 'responsibility', 'fairness', and 'efficiency'. Moreover, 'The Code' mandated that the government abide by clearly stated objectives and rules. The Blair government's unwavering commitment to sound fiscal management led the cabinet ministers to embrace periodical Comprehensive Spending Reviews (CSRs). These CSRs provided explicit departmental spending plans and objectives that were developed in accordance with strict cost–benefit calculations. 'Comprehensive Spending Reviews' and 'public service agreements' were subsequently established to assess the most efficient use of resources in an effort to eliminate waste and inefficiency. Additionally, a 'Performance Innovation Unit' (PIU) was set up to ensure greater coherence in policy design and implementation.

In order to restrict the propensity for 'excessive' public borrowing, the Blair government also implemented what became known as the 'Golden Rule'—which placed strict limits on public debt to no more than 40 per cent of the GDP. Accordingly, Blair assured the business community that his government would not engage in further deficit spending for health, education, or social security. Blair's welfare reform package included a new welfare-to-work programme that was directly modelled on Clinton's version of 'workfare'. Initially financed through a one-time 'windfall tax' on privatized utilities, Blair's training-based welfare reform experiment was consistent with his public commitment to 'social justice' as well as his election promise that welfare benefits be distributed in accordance with new standards ensuring individual 'accountability' and 'responsibility'.

To sum up, Blair's social policy reform agenda focused on three essential areas: (1) unemployment benefits, (2) subsidies for the working poor, and (3) the National Health Service (NHS). Largely inspired by Thatcher's bold NPM-based reforms of the welfare state, Blair's new initiatives were focused on streamlining administrative functions and procedures in order to make them more efficient. New measures of accountability and transparency were enacted in these sectors to ensure successful compliance. Following Thatcher's line of reasoning, Blair argued that simply providing 'more money' was not sufficient to address the deeper structural problems embedded in Britain's ailing welfare system. Accordingly, the neoliberal prime minister sought to replace Britain's 'paternalistic' welfare system with a more 'flexibilist' workfare training scheme that was consistent with NPM 'partnership' models with private organizations.

Originating as a political backlash against Keynesian 'big government', the first wave of the NPM found great sympathy within the Reagan and Thatcher governments. In a few short years, there seemed to be a pandemic: NPM ideas had taken hold of governments around the world. However, as we saw, various aspects of the NPM approach were emphasized by different leaders in different countries. The common thread connecting them was their joint emphasis on greater 'efficiency' and the imposition of performance-based accountability standards and practices. Ironically, stronger (not weaker) government intervention, in some instances, was required to institutionalize this market-based paradigm in the administrative structures and processes at various governing levels throughout these countries. It is remarkable that some of the most spectacular expressions of the NPM were vigorously undertaken by democratic Left governments in Australia during the 1970s and in the US and Britain during the 1990s. Today the NPM's emphasis on customer service, management by objectives, and quantitative-based performance and accountability standards is evident in nearly every organizational mission statement and political conversation involving the public sector. Indeed, the unquestionable adoption of NPM-based principles now evident at all levels of governance suggests that there is no alternative to this style of management. But is there no alternative? New movements in public administration, which have surfaced during recent years, have been challenging this view.

Chapter 6
The new administrative age

From 'best practices' to 'reflective practice'

As we saw in Chapter 5, important NPM reforms were undertaken by various governments that had focused on instituting private business-style performance and accountability standards. A number of these quantitative-based performance standards were adopted in the name of promoting efficiency and increasing organizational performance. In focusing exclusively on the so called 'bottom-line', however, many of these approaches failed to address deeper systemic or structural issues underlying the actual causes of poor performance. As a result, a variety of alternative methods and approaches have been gaining popularity in the field and practice of public administration over the last few decades. Introduced by Donald Schon and others, reflective practice, for example, has been gaining a strong foothold in the areas of organizational management. Reflective practice hinges upon the ongoing exercise of self-assessment of what a given manager may be 'doing right, what he/she may be doing wrong, and what he/she could be doing better'. Organizational members learn while doing so that they can make improvements to existing practices and methods in real time. Only organizational leaders at the highest levels, however, have the power to create a 'learning by doing culture' within their respective agencies. This means that employees must be given the

Table 3 Characteristics of a learning organization

	Supports innovation	Does not support/Suppresses innovation
Aims	Stakeholder, societal benefit, learning	Primarily financial benefit
Objectives	Organizational	Narrow functional
Structure	Heterarchy, adaptable interaction across functions	Hierarchy, rigid functional reporting
Internal relationships	Collaborative, cross-functional	Competitive
Rewards, recognition	Non-competitive, celebrates organizational accomplishments	Zero-sum, competitive, focused on the individual, based on executing assignments and meeting targets

Treatment of failure	Treated as opportunity for learning, value placed on knowing what doesn't work, culture of intelligent risk-taking	Punishment, criticism
Treatment of success	Teamwork recognized, contribution to greater good celebrated	Ascribed to individuals
Time horizon	Long term as well as short term	Short term only
Basis for evaluation of investments	Consideration of potential markets, customers, competitors as well as financial evaluation	Use of common financial tools alone
Exploration for ideas	Wide-ranging search for new technologies and processes	Restricted to study of recognized within-industry competition
Experimentation	Encouraged, supported by education and training, time and coaching provided	Not recognized as a valuable practice

Source: Gipsie Ranney, slide presentation on 'Deming's Ideas in the Twenty-first Century', The In2In Network Forum Meetings at California State University Northridge on 20 June 2014.

freedom and flexibility by their leaders and managers within the organization to take risks and engage in experimentation.

Leaders who have taken the initiative to create so-called 'learning organization' cultures typically encourage employees to reflect upon both positive and negative feedback that results from the decisions that they make and the actions that they take. Moreover, conflicts and dilemmas in such organizations are resolved through frank and honest discussions among managers and their subordinates. Leadership and innovation specialist Gipsie B. Ranney has identified some of the key characteristics of a learning organization that are shared in Table 3.

The 'New Economics' and systems learning

In the closing sentence of his widely read book, *The New Economics for Industry, Government & Education*, W. Edwards Deming asserted that management processes that overemphasize 'conformance to specifications, zero defects, Six Sigma Quality, and other specifications-based nostrums all miss the point'. At a glance Deming's carefully selected comments might appear to be a scathing condemnation of NPM-style quantitative performance measures. However, this surely was not the case. Rather, Deming sought to re-direct management's narrow emphasis on technical measures of performance to the importance of adopting a wider philosophy of leadership. Efficiency, Deming reasoned, means doing something 'right', while effective leadership, he went on to argue, involves doing the 'right thing' in the first place. Accordingly, Deming insisted that leaders must possess a clear vision and be able to effectively communicate that vision to the other members in the organization.

Proceeding according to the belief that no agency operates in complete isolation, Deming asserted that well-functioning organizations characteristically perform their tasks and duties as part of an overall 'system' in the service of a common purpose.

Traditional organizational cultures, by way of contrast, focus on improving the parts of a system (i.e. individual agency and departments there within), rather than focusing on the agency's function within an interdependent system of other organizations. In Deming's view, 'a system is a network of interdependent components' that work in unison to accomplish specified aims outlined and supported by organizational leaders. To illustrate this, Deming compared a manager within an organization to a conductor of an orchestra. The role of the conductor, in Deming's illustration, is to get the individual musicians to perform as part of a larger symphony. If the most talented violinist fails to perform in synchronicity with the rest of the orchestra, the performance will be ruined. Indeed, in order to be successful, musicians must work together interdependently in a manner where each member supports the others and vice versa. To help us better understand the importance of leadership in shaping a system that fosters trust and cooperation rather than undermines them, Deming outlined his illustrious 'Fourteen Points' of effective organizations, which can be seen in Box 9.

Failure on the part of public administrators to properly comprehend how their work may be interdependent with the functions performed by other agencies can have catastrophic consequences. To illustrate this point, let us briefly look at one high profile case related to child welfare and safety. In Los Angeles County, the administration of child welfare depends upon the complex interaction and joint involvement of multiple county agencies and countless administrators. The Department of Family and Children Services (DCFS), the Department of Mental Health, the Department of Social Services, local school districts, the county sheriff's department, as well as the district attorney's office and the family courts are jointly involved in the process of assessing the well-being of a child who has been placed under the county's oversight. While each of these agencies (and the departments within them) perform a number of important functions that are interrelated to one another in this assessment

Box 9 W. Edwards Deming's 'fourteen points' of effective organizations

1. Create constancy of purpose toward improvement of service.
2. Management must assume leadership for change.
3. Eliminate the need for inspection on a mass basis; build quality into the process in the first place.
4. Minimize total cost. Move toward a single supplier for any one item or service; build a long-term relationship of loyalty and trust.
5. A focus on continuous improvement of the system will result in the continuous reduction of costs.
6. Institute an ongoing programme of 'training on the job'.
7. The goal of management should be to support subordinates to do a better job.
8. Drive out fear, so that everyone may work effectively for the organization.
9. Break down barriers between departments and help them to work as a team.
10. Eliminate management by objective and other numerical goals. The causes of low productivity belong to the system and thus lie beyond the power of the employees.
11. Remove barriers that deprive the employee of his/her right to pride of service.
12. Remove barriers that deprive managers of their right to pride of service.
13. Institute a vigorous programme of education and self-improvement.
14. Put everybody in the organization to work to accomplish the transformation.

Source: Adapted from: The W. Edwards Deming Institute and W. Edwards Deming, *Out of the Crisis*.

and protection process, they often carry out their duties as though they are unconnected.

In the most extreme instances, failure to coordinate and share information among agencies can be fatal. From 2009 to 2013, three children died while under the supervision of the Los Angeles child welfare system. Just as concerning, a Blue Ribbon Commission, appointed by the county to investigate the cause behind these tragic deaths, found that dozens of other cases of child abuse that had been reported had not been properly investigated by the pertinent agencies. Citing poor inter-agency communication and coordination, the Commission's report revealed that the tragedy was the result of a systems-wide reporting failure. Many of these child welfare cases 'fell through the cracks' between agencies that were supposed to be coordinating with one another. Following the release of the Commission's report, the LA County DCFS agency director confirmed that 'there are a lot of challenges in the county [such] that no one agency can be totally responsible for child protection... Health and mental health and DCFS and probation and law enforcement and a whole host of other organizations, private included, have to be responsible for child protection'.

As we can see from the heartbreaking example just given, communication is essential to inter-agency cooperation. However, in order for genuine communication among public administrators operating across different agencies to occur, they must develop a shared awareness of how their respective duties and functions are interconnected. In reality, however, conversations among public sector organizations operating across county, regional, and state jurisdictions are rare. Closed organizational cultures often keep managers from seeing how their respective functions and duties may depend upon the work of others operating outside agencies. Indeed, most traditional top–down command-and-control organizational cultures have detrimental 'blind spots' that may keep their leaders and managers from seeing their many common problems, threats, opportunities, and financial resources as shared phenomena (in those cases where they may actually exist).

While the benefits of inter-agency cooperation should be obvious, cultivating pathways that facilitate communication and ongoing dialogues among different public agencies is no easy task. That said, inter-agency linkages are most easily facilitated through personal and professional interactions of their employees. For example, many deep and enduring professional bonds can be created when employees from different agencies interact with one another through common education and training experiences. To examine in more depth how this process works let us look at a case where a group of management-bound employees from separate organizations shared common post-graduate professional education.

A few years ago the Los Angeles County's chief administrative officer led an initiative to explore ways in which innovative training and degree-based programmes could be developed to provide mid-career county employees with the essential skill sets required to meet new challenges facing their public agencies. As a result of these discussions, the county began working collaboratively with one local university to deliver graduate degree and training classes on-site at various county agencies through a 'student cohort' learning model. County employees who enrolled in the university's Master's degree cohort in public administration (MPA) would take the same classes together for two years. Through intensive classroom discussion and group interaction, cohort members gradually developed an acute awareness of how their own work was interdependent with the work of others outside their own organizational divisions and agencies. Perhaps most importantly, students engaged in substantive discussions related to how they could apply both the academic and practical organizational knowledge that they had shared over their time in the classroom to improve communication and coordination among their own agencies.

The New Public Service

Having examined how systems thinking may work in theory and practice, let us look at another emergent public administration approach that has been gaining attention in recent years. Originating out of a fundamental philosophical dispute with core tenets of NPM approaches regarding the prime purpose of government and the public sector, a new paradigm known as the 'New Public Service' (NPS) first appeared at the beginning of the 21st century. Seeking to address 'core questions about the nature of public service, the role of administration in governance and the value tensions surrounding bureaucracy, efficiency, responsiveness, and accountability', its leading proponents, Janet Denhardt and Robert Denhardt, emphasized civic oriented virtues over business principles. Governance, they argue, needs to be focused first and foremost on creating 'public value', a term first coined by Harvard management professor Mark H. Moore of the Kennedy School of Government. The NPS's emphasis on creating public value has been gaining attention in the field and practice of public administration over the last two decades. Creating public value involves encouraging citizens to get more directly involved in establishing collective goals and then working with them to develop strategies for achieving them. According to management expert John Bryson, this means 'producing enterprises, policies, programmes, projects, services, or physical, technological, social, political, and cultural infrastructure that advance the public interest and the common good at a reasonable cost'.

It is incumbent on public managers to develop innovative ways for building greater citizen trust in their public institutions. In that endeavour, public managers must pose several essential questions. These include: for what purpose was this organization originally created? Why does it continue to exist? Who does it serve? How do we know if this organization has been successful in maximizing the public values and related policy goals that were established cooperatively by the citizens and the public sector organizations that serve them? (See Box 10.)

Adopting the buzz-phrase 'service rather than steering', Denhardt and Denhardt sought to replace NPM's rather narrow focus on 'efficiency' (and concepts related to it) with values like 'democratic accountability' and 'citizen engagement'. The NPS is premised on the belief that giving citizens greater access to the political-policy process, and affording them a genuine voice in shaping these processes in the first place, would help them become personally invested in creating meaningful change in their own communities. Through a process known as 'deliberative governance', policy and administrative decisions are reached through consensus-building discussions with citizens operating on

> **Box 10 Core tenets of the New Public Service**
>
> 1. The role of public servants is to help citizens realize their shared interests rather than steering society in new directions.
> 2. Public needs can be most effectively achieved through collective efforts and collaborative processes and shared leadership.
> 3. The public interest is the result of a dialogue about shared values rather than the aggregation of individual self-interest.
> 4. Public servants should not merely respond to the demands of customers, but rather build relationships based on citizen trust.
> 5. Public servants must attend to statutory and constitutional law, community values, political norms, professional standards, and citizen interests.
>
> Source: Robert B. Denhardt, Janet V. Denhardt, and Maria P. Aristigueta, *Managing Human Behavior in Public and Nonprofit Organizations*, pp. 467–70.

the same level as government officials, policy experts, business people, the media, and other pertinent interests. Under the NPS governance model, citizens are treated as 'stakeholders' who are actively involved in defining problems and helping craft solutions that reflect the unique conditions and features that shape the communities in which they reside. In stressing the importance of democratic values and participatory-based governance, the NPS is, in many ways, highly sympathetic to Dwight Waldo's New Public Administration (NPA) approach that we mentioned in Chapter 5.

One tool that is being used to facilitate and help structure such discussions involving numerous stakeholders is a deliberative process known as a 'strategic planning cycle' (sometimes called a 'strategy change cycle'). A strategic planning cycle is a more open and generally more inclusive type of strategic planning model that is particularly well-suited for use in the public and non-profit sectors. Often structured much more organically and informally than traditional top–down strategic planning approaches, strategic planning cycles are especially useful for helping public managers supervise how and when different stakeholders may participate in multistage deliberative planning processes. As part of this process, a stakeholder analysis is often employed to help participants develop a better understanding of the political, social, and economic environment surrounding the organization. Having an improved understanding of how the public organization is positioned within the broader system will prove extremely useful in assisting public managers identify important strategic issues and problems facing them and their constituent-clients. Employing principles of reflective practice discussed earlier, these public managers can use this vital information to improve the decisions that they make and the actions that follow.

As public managers transition to their new roles as facilitators and honest brokers between 'the people' and government agencies, they will have to become skilled in building unconventional partnerships with diverse groups of citizens when designing and implementing solutions to ever complex global problems. At the same time, the success of the NPS model depends upon the active participation of well-informed citizens who are equipped to engage in deep policy debates. Simply affording greater access to citizens to participate in the governing process is not sufficient. Citizens must become conversant with the important political issues facing society as well as the policy and administrative process related to them.

Critics of the NPS, however, point out that most lay citizens in the United States do not possess the knowledge of public policy (and its related processes) or expert administrative skills needed to successfully carry out 'public work' in a manner that creates 'public value'. According to *The Economist* magazine's well-respected Democracy Index, some countries are much better suited to NPS-style participatory forms of governance than others. Compiled by The Economist Intelligence Unit, the Index employs sixty separate indicators to rank over 160 countries according to their democratic status. Taking into account an extensive list of factors that fall under the general categories of (1) electoral process, (2) civil liberties, (3) functioning of government, (4) political participation, and (5) political culture, the index is one of the most comprehensive measures of its kind. According to the Index, countries like Norway, Sweden, and Iceland might appear to fare better with respect to the qualities required for NPS governance processes to work successfully, whereas a country that may rank further down the list, such as the United States, might be less likely to do so.

Even if a given country possesses the 'correct' mix of factors that would make them ripe candidates for NPS, these critics go on to point out, this still leaves us with unresolved questions regarding what it means to 'create public value' in the first place. Indeed, 'what is it' and 'who gets to define it' are burning issues that NPS advocates are still debating.

Chapter 7
Globalization and the rise of network governance

The world is changing—and changing fast! As public administration continues to evolve in the globalization era, many of the problems contemporary governments must confront domestically originate in countries and regions outside their borders. Constrained in their ability to directly tackle such problems at their foreign source, local public administrators must adapt to working in environments that are increasingly unstable and hence much less predictable. Indeed, a new era characterized by 'unreason' and 'confusion' where 'no one is in charge' is quickly eclipsing 'rationalized' processes that have characteristically been associated with the relatively stable nation-state-centric system.

Many of the administrative activities associated with public governance and administration, which traditionally fell under the control of nation-states, are now being carried out by loosely knit networks of governmental and non-governmental organizations (NGOs), private corporations, independent agencies, and citizen groups. Usually organized around a specific set of related policies or administrative issues or concerns, such international networks may include individuals and groups operating simultaneously at the local, regional, national, and international levels. Commonly referred to as 'network governance' or 'governance by network', the participation of multiple domestic and international actors can frustrate the efforts of sovereign governing authorities to successfully implement public policy. Forced to operate under such multifarious environments, contemporary public managers are compelled to develop new consensus-building skill sets in order to bring otherwise disparate sets of domestic and international groups together in the pursuit of collective goals. Let us look at some of these network approaches in more depth.

As we have discussed, the forces of globalization are compelling public administrators to direct their attention increasingly towards transnational forms of governance. Here again, traditional top–down organizational systems are poorly structured to address complex global problems and crises requiring international cooperation. In the last few decades loosely organized networks of public and private agencies operating through multiple layers of government have been playing an increasing role in public administration.

In network-governance-type systems, power and authority tends to be decentralized and dispersed among a variety of autonomous stakeholders operating beyond the scope and control of national governments. Organized around values, concerns, issues, and problems ranging from global climate change to human security, governing networks can vary widely in their size and scope. Flexible and fluid in their organizational structure, they allow participants to flow in-and-out of a network as circumstances change. In order to address a given terrorist threat emanating from abroad, for example, the United States Department of Homeland Security must communicate and coordinate with domestic organizations such as the FBI, CIA, NSA, and local police agencies as well as with international intelligence agencies such as INTERPOL. As circumstances surrounding the threat may change, new partnerships may be forged with other agencies and groups. Let us now look at some examples of how governing networks organized at the municipal, regional, and national levels have been particularly influential in addressing the climate change crisis (Box 11).

Box 11 Types of policy and administrative networks

1. *Informational*: Members share ideas and knowledge, which they use to inform their own work in their home organizations.
2. *Developmental*: Members exchange information and ideas. Educational resources provided to assist employees develop capacities to improve performance.
3. *Outreach*: In addition to helping members engage in informational and developmental activities, network members share client contact information and resource opportunities.
4. *Action*: Members work to alter their home organization's policies and routines to help achieve the network's common goals. Formal collaborations include sharing of funds, service delivery, or development of common resources for the network's future use.

Source: Robert Agranoff, Managing Within Networks: Adding Value to Public Organizations, p. 10.

Today the majority of the world's seven billion people live in cities and other large metropolitan areas. Not surprisingly, the world's largest cities are responsible for producing most of the world's waste and pollution. More specifically, large metropolitan regions now collectively produce more than two thirds of the world's CO_2 emissions—the main cause of global climate change. Encumbered by the large size of their bureaucracies and onerous political processes, national governments have characteristically been slow to respond with substantive policy changes and administrative action. Diminishing national power associated with recent globalization trends has emboldened municipal and regional agencies across the world to assume a leading role in reducing their aggregate CO_2 levels. A number of local leaders and administrators representing the world's largest cities have been collaborating through organizations known as 'transnational municipal networks' (TMNs) to accomplish this goal. Comprised of subnational governments that have partnered with international organizations and private corporations, politically powerful TMNs, such as the World Association of Major Metropolises, and international development organizations, such as the United Nations Conference on Environment and Development (UNCED), have been highly successful in mobilizing cross-national efforts to address climate change and related challenges confronting major urban areas. Originating with only three cities in 1992, UNCED had swelled during less than two decades to over one hundred members. Keen that his own city should take the lead on this pressing issue, London's mayor, Ken Livingstone, founded a consortium of major municipalities that later become known as the C40. Today one of the most influential municipal-based networks governing the issue of climate change, the C40 employs a variety of market and planning instruments to circumvent traditionally rigid and formal state-centric bureaucracies. Having grown to nearly seventy cities of various sizes and scope, the C40 successfully collaborated with the World Bank in 2011 to establish 'a common standard for measuring greenhouse gas emissions'. The C40 claimed victory when these standards were adopted by the Bank's Climate Investment Fund to help better inform their funding and investment decisions.

City leaders are not the only ones who have been tapping into international networks to combat the causes of global climate change. State and regional leaders in the United States, for example, have initiated governing networks of their own. Determined to make timely and substantive policy strides to reduce CO_2 levels in the Western region of the United States, Arizona Governor Janet Napolitano boldly proclaimed that 'in the absence of meaningful federal action, it is up to the states to take action to address climate change and reduce greenhouse gas emissions in the country'. Alarmed that Western states were 'being particularly hard hit by the effects of climate change' the Arizona leader joined five other regional governors from California, Oregon, New Mexico, and Washington in imposing strict regional limits on greenhouse gas emissions. To make sure that more heavily industrialized states were treated proportionately, the enterprising group adopted a regional 'cap and trade' scheme which would allow member states to purchase and sell CO_2 emissions credits that kept within these regional limits. In 2009, California's Governor Arnold Schwarzenegger hosted a global climate change summit in cooperation with the United Nations Development Programme (UNDP) and the United Nations Environment Programme (UNEP) to develop cooperative initiatives to promote sustainable energy production and use. The conference was impressively attended by more than thirty governors, local officials, business leaders, and policy experts representing more than seventy states and provinces from all over the world.

International networks are becoming important players in transnational water governance in the developing world as well. The overexploitation and excessive contamination of vital water sources has created public health and sustainability crises in parts of Asia, Africa, and Latin America. In its inaugural Water Development Report released in 2003, the United Nations pronounced that the 'water crisis is essentially a crisis of governance and societies are facing a number of social, economic and political challenges on how to govern water more effectively'. Relatedly, the World Summit on Sustainable Development emphasized the importance of developing private–public sector partnerships to carry out the administrative functions related to the regulation, maintenance, and distribution of essential water resources.

Over the last two decades India's national government has undertaken bold privatization initiatives to improve water management throughout the country. As part of this effort, the country's federal and state governments have been partnering with international financial institutions (such as the World Bank and Asian Development Bank), private sector firms, and NGOs. In a monumental effort to modernize the country's antiquated water infrastructure, the Central Ministry of Urban Development eliminated protectionist barriers against Foreign Direct Investment (FDI) funding for new capital projects and removed import restrictions on foreign-sourced potable water facilities and equipment. Relatedly, the Confederation of Indian Industry (CII) and the Indian Business Alliance on Water (IBAW) have been working collaboratively with international agencies such as the UNDP and the United States Agency for International Development (USAID) in broadening business-sector participation and engagement. India's central government has simultaneously been working with international expert consultants operating out of Geneva, Stockholm, and Washington, DC, to provide much needed technical and administrative expertise related to the monitoring and distribution of potable water.

Let us wind up our discussion on network governance with a brief examination of how information technologies have been shaping new patterns of administrative processes. Governments around the globe have been adopting new information and communication technologies (ICTs) to improve administrative efficiency consistent with NPM principles as well as strengthen citizen–government relationships in line with democratic values emphasized by the NPS. The phenomenon known popularly as 'e-governance' is reshaping public administration as we have known it. In its general usage, the term 'e-governance' refers to the various uses of information technology related to public sector governance. Relatedly, management experts Grant and Chau suggest that the core purposes of e-governance are '(1) to develop and deliver high quality, seamless, and integrated public services; (2) to enable effective constituent relationship management; and (3) to support the economic and social development goals of citizens, businesses, and civil society at local, state, national, and international levels'.

Recognizing that its industrial competitiveness was dependent upon creating continuous and unlimited access to publicly maintained sources of information, in 2000 the Swedish government passed a historic law promising 'An Information Society for All'. In an effort to dismantle administrative divides between organizations, the Swedish Public Management Agency adopted a comprehensive ICT programme to transform traditional hierarchical public agencies into so-called 'e-networked' open agencies. Today, national and local governments all over the industrialized world have followed Sweden's lead by investing heavily in e-governance infrastructure to promote open access to public information resulting in improved democratic oversight and accountability. As a result, citizens enjoy virtually unlimited access to public records and official government documents such as property tax records, historical maps, minutes from public hearings, and public employee salaries.

Managing and protecting the personal data of citizens contained within many public documents, however, has proven to be a daunting challenge for administrators operating at all levels of government. Integrating separate sources of public information and making them widely available can pose serious threats to personal privacy. A number of countries have responded by passing strict laws governing how public administrators may handle, transmit, share, store, and access certain kinds of sensitive information. At the same time, as noted earlier, in many specific instances it is essential that public employees and citizens alike are afforded access to vast information systems and databases managed by public sector organizations. Consequently, these systems are particularly vulnerable to attacks initiated by Internet hackers and criminal networks. Indeed, untold amounts of taxpayer dollars and countless manpower hours are now expended on security systems and employee data management training to reduce these threats. Criminal attacks on public agency data systems are costing countries and their subnational governments hundreds of millions of dollars per year.

In various forms and guises, governing networks have been playing a major role in public administration. The notion of the 'modern state', as established at Westphalia, and its traditional means and methods of providing public services are being redefined. New forms of public–private 'collaborative' relationships have been emerging in its place. A new breed of reflective public managers must be groomed with new skill sets if they are to lead their organizations through ever-shifting global environments. As we have seen, governing networks can serve a number of important functions in a democratic society. Innovation, for example, is often facilitated through supplemental knowledge and expertise through the participation of institutions and individuals that operate outside of the official offices of government. Moreover, owing to their fluid and flexible organizational structure, networks can adapt and respond quickly to pressing problems immediately as they arise. At the same time, however, given their highly complex and decentralized structure, organizational goals and objectives can become blurred and convoluted. Moreover, official oversight of public goods and services, formally provided by governments, can no longer be guaranteed when administrative processes are transferred to either the private sector or semi-public institutions. With government no longer at the helm to steer the policy and administrative process, public accountability and responsibility can easily be sacrificed.

Chapter 8
The future of public administration

As we have seen, both the field and the practice of public administration have been extraordinarily dynamic. Therefore, their future is impossible to predict. While essential public services, ranging from waste management to public education, are not likely to disappear any time soon, the manner in which their administrative functions are carried out and evaluated is likely to change considerably. As we have seen in our brief journey, dramatic changes taking place at the global level are bringing radical shifts in public administration. Unable to shield their domestic political, economic, and social affairs from the powerful effects of globalization, public managers are forced to perform their functions and mandates in highly unstable and capricious environments. Hoping to attract new global financial investment, modern governments have been engaged in a fierce 'race to the bottom' to slash their public budgets. In a globalized world characterized by growing 'uncertainty', the politics of budgetary austerity is pressing on public administrators at every level of government. They must think in radically different ways about what it means to govern in the 21st century.

Following the global financial crisis that surfaced in 2008, the Public Sector Research Centre (PSRC), established by PricewaterhouseCoopers, published a report entitled 'The Road Ahead for Public Service Delivery'. This outlined specific core capabilities that government agencies would have to develop in order to be successful over the long term. Besides emphasizing 'public-private partnerships, co-venturing, co-creation and co-design' as '"must-have" capabilities', the report also stressed that public organizations should become increasingly 'agile, interconnected, and transparent'. It called upon public sector leaders to become the essential 'change agents' in this process. Emphasizing systems-oriented leadership over traditional task-focused management, it urged public sector leaders to articulate a new vision for their agencies. Consistent with the goals advanced by the New Public Service, the PSRC report emphasized citizen-oriented service as the highest public sector priority. Therefore, the focus of government efforts should be directed above all at 'energizing' both internal and external stakeholders. They should encourage public administrators to work in partnership with the citizens they serve, so as to identify civic problems and devise innovative solutions.

Today's public administrators are challenged to meet the growing expectations of a demanding citizenry. The British market research firm Ipsos MORI conducted a 'public services satisfaction' survey of 5,000 citizens across ten countries. It revealed that 41 per cent of US citizens were 'dissatisfied' with the way public services were administered and managed by the government. Interestingly this was markedly different from countries such as Australia, Brazil, Canada, France, Germany, India, Italy, Singapore, and the United Kingdom, where the level of 'satisfied' respondents averaged nearly 65 per cent. When questioned what they believed the most important focus of government ought to be, the majority of US respondents expressed that they wanted government to 'provide services in a more cost effective way'. Curiously, while US citizens between 50 and 64 'reported the highest levels of dissatisfaction' with the cost and quality of government-provided services, those under 35 were optimistic that the US government would be able to meet their 'needs and expectations over the next five years'. The survey further revealed that citizens, in general, expect to see significant improvements in the way public services are administered in today's 'high-touch' society. Besides demanding greater personalized service, citizen demands for increased 'transparency' and 'accountability' in public sector governance have been growing increasingly abrasive.

The next decade

As we saw in Chapter 7, access to a growing number of government services and information is being made available to average citizens, twenty-four hours a day, through new forms of e-governance. Indeed, the explosion of Internet-based services has provided diverse public agencies with new methods of interacting directly with their citizens. At the same time, however, increased access to the policy and administrative process can be a double-edged sword. With greater access comes increased scrutiny of the policy and administrative process. Critics charge, for example, that once the political door is opened to the voices of disgruntled individuals, emotionally charged popular opinion will replace sober policy discussion and reasoned debate.

Under the guise of creating 'leaner and meaner' forms of government, right-of-centre political movements in countries like the United States have been waging a political assault on the public sector. Still, as we have seen, in a number of nations questions related to the changing role of the civil service sector tend to be less adversarial, or at least much less partisan, than in others. Despite relentless rhetorical assaults on 'big government', the role of the public sector has not been diminished significantly. Indeed, recent data confirms that public sector spending continues to steadily increase. In the US, for example, public expenditure now accounts for 42 per cent of GDP, compared to only 28 per cent in 1960. While there was a slight decrease from 2009 to 2014 in the years immediately following the global financial crisis, the overall trend indicates that public sector spending will continue to grow. Also worthy of note, government revenues (as a percentage of the country's gross domestic product) have declined. This, in turn, has placed unprecedented strains on public agencies and the administrators who serve in them. As challenges related to immigration, global climate change, exotic disease outbreaks, and so forth grow ever more complex in the future, the burden on public administrators can only be expected to increase. (For a historical overview of the growth of public expenditures, see Figure 3.)

The world's population is now estimated at over seven billion people and continues to increase. Some studies project that it could reach eight billion within ten years. Increases in life expectancy rates, changes in family structure, and growing levels of unemployment have compelled policymakers in the US to respond with a host of new public services and additional levels of welfare support. As waves of so-called baby-boomers move toward retirement, there will be unprecedented pressure on public pensions and healthcare systems. At present, nearly 15 per cent of US citizens are over 65. This number is projected to increase to over 18 per cent within ten years. This means that nearly one in five citizens will be eligible for public retirement benefits. At present, over 90 per cent of senior citizens in the US receive

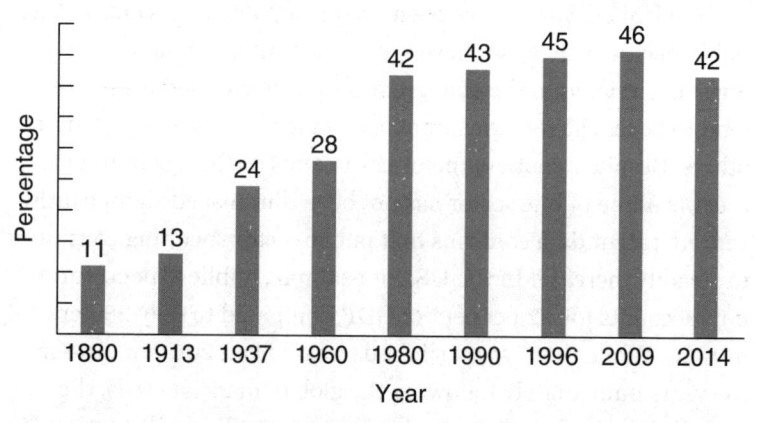

3. Government expenditure as a percentage of GDP, high income countries and OECD nations, 1880–2014.

Medicare entitlement benefits, which currently cost the country's taxpayers more than $500 billion a year. By 2015, according to the PSRC Report, the combined federal, state, and local costs required to fund public services for the country's growing elderly population are estimated to reach as high as $940 billion (4.4 per cent of GDP) a year.

The recent European financial crisis of 2015 has exposed deep structural weaknesses that have long been embedded in the continent's southern economies of Greece, Spain, and Portugal. In addition to having to confront the challenges associated with chronic youth unemployment, governments in these countries are being forced to expand public services for growing numbers of retirees. Indeed, the proportional size of the senior citizen population is increasing dramatically in advanced industrial countries all over the world.

Unfortunately, most strategic discussions and debates among policymakers and public administrators on how best to avert crises before they happen (and address them once they occur) tend to be crafted in mutually exclusive ideological terms such as 'governments versus markets'. These false dichotomies fail to provide policymakers and administrators with useful lenses for identifying problems. As a result, they often prohibit them from devising pragmatic solutions. Public officials and administrators ought to be focused on developing sufficient government-led regulatory institutions and policies required to support well-functioning markets.

The health and vitality of any given country's public sector is closely tied to the conditions of its private economy. Called 'the greatest recession since the Great Depression' (of the 1930s), the devastating global financial meltdown of 2008 will have long-term effects that remain unknown. Current US practices of borrowing from the future to pay for public programmes and services are not sustainable over the long term. At the same time, eviscerating essential public services and programmes, as in many European countries, can have dire consequences. The social safety net provided through pensions, public healthcare services, public education, and social insurance can only be retracted so far without disturbing the legitimacy of democratic governments throughout Europe.

There is no question that the future will usher in new sets of challenges for the nation-state and its public administration systems. Some argue that these challenges are placing public servants in untenable positions. Others, however, claim that they are creating historic opportunities for public administrators to create meaningful and positive change. In the past, administrative reforms were characteristically shaped in accordance with each nation's unique social structure, institutional configurations, and historical traditions. In recent years, however, we have witnessed rapid global, economic, and social changes that are challenging traditional administrative norms and practices. The most important focus of public management and leadership, therefore, should be the hiring of the 'right' individuals with the 'right' skill sets required to meet the enormous challenges confronting our civilization in the global age.

References and further reading

In keeping within the tight scope of the VSI standard, we limited our brief overview to some of the key highlights in the field and practice of public administration. It was not our intention to cover all of the topics, approaches, and concepts associated with this very broad and dynamic subject in this introductory narrative. Indeed, the field of public administration is awash with excellent handbooks, textbooks, monographs, and scholarly publications that cover specific topics and approaches with the full depth and breadth that they command. We have been greatly inspired by many of them in crafting this introductory narrative. In keeping with the general style of Oxford's *Very Short Introduction* series, we have used direct quotations sparingly and most are referenced in the textboxes that appear throughout. Having gained a basic understanding of the topics discussed here, most readers will be sufficiently prepared to move on to more advanced books and articles.

Chapter 1: A contemporary overview

There are a number of solid textbooks that survey the concepts, theories, and approaches of public administration. The following are particularly strong in this regard: Jay M. Shafritz and J. Steven Ott, *Classics of Organization Theory*, 8th edn (Harcourt, 2015); Jay M. Shafritz and Albert C. Hyde, *Classics of Public Administration*, 7th edn (Wadsworth, 2011); Janet Denhardt and Robert Denhardt, *Public Administration: An Action Orientation*, 6th edn (Wadsworth Publishing, 2008); J. Steven Ott and Edward W. Russell, *Introduction to Public Administration: A Book of Readings* (Longman, 2001);

Christopher Hood, *The Art of the State: Culture, Rhetoric and Public Management* (Oxford University Press, 1998); George H. Frederickson, *The Spirit of Public Administration* (Jossey-Bass, 1996).

Classical sources on the origins and workings of government include: Frank Goodnow, *Politics and Administration: A Study in Government* (Classic Reprint) (Forgotten Books, 2012); Herbert Simon, *Administrative Behavior: A Study of Decision-Making Processes in Administrative Organization*, 3rd edn (Free Press, 1976).

A seminal book on the public policy process is Daniel Mazmanian and Paul Sabatier, *Implementation and Public Policy* (University Press of America, 1989). For a very readable overview of the policy process, please see Stella Z. Theodoulou and Chris Kofinis, *The Art of the Game: Understanding American Public Policy Making* (Wadsworth, 2004).

Some important works on bureaucracy and public management include: James Q. Wilson, *Bureaucracy* (Basic Books, 1989); Guy B. Peters, *The Politics of Bureaucracy: An Introduction to Comparative Public Administration*, 6th edn (Routledge, 2009); Laurence E. Lynn, Jr and Sydney Stein, Jr, *Public Management: Old and New* (Routledge, 2006); Allison Graham and Philip Zelikow, *Essence of Decision: Explaining the Cuban Missile Crisis*, 2nd edn (Pearson, 1999); James Q. Wilson, *What Government Agencies Do and Why They Do It* (Basic Books, 1991); William A. Niskanen, Jr, *Bureaucracy and Representative Government* (Aldine, 1971).

For a solid understanding of public administration systems from a global perspective, we recommend: Jos Raadschelders and Eran Vigoda-Gadot, *Global Dimensions of Public Administration and Governance: A Comparative Voyage* (John Wiley & Sons, 2015); J. A. Chandler, *Comparative Public Administration* (Routledge, 2014); Evan M. Berman, *Public Administration in East Asia: Mainland China, Japan, South Korea* (Taiwan CRC Press, 2010); Ali Farazmand, 'State tradition and public administration in Iran in ancient and modern times', in Ali Farazmand (ed.), *Handbook of Comparative and Development Public Administration* (Marcel Dekker, 1991); Georgije Ostrogorski, *History of the Byzantine State* (Rutgers University Press, 1969).

For an alternative take on pre-modern leadership in society, please see Christopher Boehm, *Hierarchy in the Forest* (Harvard University Press, 1999).

The quote from John T. Harvey was drawn from his essay 'Why government should not be run like a business' that appeared in the 'Leadership' section of *Forbes* (online), 5 October 2012: <http://www.forbes.com/sites/johntharvey/2012/10/05/government-vs-business/#db2541826858>.

The quote by Donald Kettl that appears in this chapter is drawn from *The Worst Is Yet to Come: Lessons from September 11 and Hurricane Katrina* (University of Pennsylvania, Fels Institute of Government: Research Service Report No. 05-01, 2005): <www.unm.edu/~marivera/.../Kettl--Katrina%20and%209-11.doc>.

The quote defining the term 'governance' is drawn from Laurence E. Lynn, Jr, Carolyn J. Heinrich, and Carolyn J. Hill, *Improving Governance: A New Logic for Empirical Research* (Georgetown University Press, 2001), p. 7.

The quote on leadership by Herbert S. Lewis was drawn from Leaders and Followers: Some Anthropological Perspectives, Addison Wesley Module in Anthropology, Philippines: Addison-Wesley Publishing, January 1, 1974, No. 50, p. 3.

Population projections for the city of Melbourne were drawn from John Dagge, 'Melbourne struggling as population booms to more than five million by 2025 and 6.5 million by 2050'. *Sunday Herald Sun.* March 25, 2012 12:00AM. <http://zincip.biz/2012/03/28/melbourne-struggling-as-population-booms-to-more-than-five-million-by-2025-and-6-5-million-by-2050-2/>

Chapter 2: The journey from Westphalia to Philadelphia

There has been a long-running debate over whether Westphalia was the watershed that created a sovereign-state-system that definitively established the legal principles of territoriality, autonomy, and self-determination. We have provided the popular historical narrative in this chapter for the purpose of introducing new students of public adminstration to the concept of state sovereignty and related concepts. For a more in-depth discussion of this complex subject, we suggest Trudy Jacobsen and Charles Sampford, *Re-envisioning Sovereignty: The End of Westphalia?* (Ashgate Press, 2013); and Stephen D. Krasner, *Sovereignty: Organized Hypocrisy* (Princeton University Press, 1999).

As we noted in the text of this chapter, our discussion of the Jeffersonian, Hamiltonian, and Madisonian traditions is indebted to Donald Kettl, *The Transformation of Governance: Public Administration for the Twenty-First Century* (JHU Press, 2015).

For an in-depth historical account of popular sovereignty, we recommend: Larry Kramer, T*he People Themselves: Popular Constitutionalism and Judicial Review* (Oxford University Press, 2004); and Edmund S. Morgan, *Inventing the People: The Rise of Popular Sovereignty in England and America* (W. W. Norton & Company, 1989).

Our discussion of the *Federalist Papers* drew, in part, from: Alexander Hamilton, 'Federalist 70', in Alexander Hamilton, James Madison, and John Jay, *The Federalist Papers* (Dover Thrift Editions, Courier Corporation, 2014); James Madison, 'Federalist 10', in Alexander Hamilton, James Madison, and John Jay, *The Federalist Papers* (Dover Thrift Editions, Courier Corporation, 2014).

For additional background of the relationship between the Jeffersonian tradition and America's Tea Party movement's position on American 'state's rights', please see David Sehat, *The Jefferson Rule: How the Founding Fathers Became Infallible and Our Politics Inflexible* (Simon and Schuster, 2015).

For a deeper understanding of the relationship between popular sovereignty and devolution, we suggest: Gerry Hassan, *Independence of the Scottish Mind: Elite Narratives, Public Spaces and the Making of a Modern Nation* (Palgrave Macmillan, 2014); and Michael Gardiner, *The Cultural Roots of British Devolution* (Edinburgh University Press, 2004).

For Henry Adams' remarks on Jefferson, please see his book *History of the United States of America* (Antiquarian Press Ltd. 1962) (1889–1891) supra note 3, at 204.

Chapter 3: Progressive reform across the globe

For additional perspectives on progressivism, we suggest: Ronald J. Pestritto and William J. Atto, *American Progressivism: A Reader* (Lexington Books, 2008); Eldon Eisenach, *Social and Political Thought of American Progressivism* (Hackett Publishing Company, 2006); Woodrow Wilson, 'The Study of Administration', *Political Science Quarterly*, 2 (1888), pp. 197–222.

Party politics and progressivism are addressed in: Glenn Hurowitz, *Fear and Courage in the Democratic Party* (Maisonneuve Press, 2007); Paul Waldman, *Being Right Is Not Enough: What Progressives Can Learn from Conservative Success* (Wiley, 2006); Peter Berkowitz, *Varieties of Progressivism in America* (Hoover Institution Press, 2004).

Considerations regarding the future of democracy can be found in: David B. Woolner and John M. Thompson (eds), *Progressivism in America: Past, Present, and Future* (Oxford University Press, 2015); Bob Pepperman Taylor, *Citizenship and Democratic Doubt: The Legacy of Progressive Thought* (University Press of Kansas, 2004); Jeffrey C. Isaac, *The Poverty of Progressivism: The Future of American Democracy in a Time of Liberal Decline* (Rowman & Littlefield Publishers, 2003).

The quote by Peter Hennessy provided in this chapter was drawn from his Founder's Day Address, Hawarden Castle, 8 July 1999, cited in the Civil Service Research Paper 03/49, House of Commons Library, May 2003.

Sources for Box 3 are: Ken Johnson, 'According to Max Weber: historical principles' in 'Busting Bureaucracy', 16 March 2016 <http://www.bustingbureaucracy.com/excerpts/weber.htm>; Stella Z. Theodoulou and Christopher Kofinis, *The Art of the Game* (Wadsworth, 2004).

For a readable overview of the 'Four Main Administrative Traditions', please see Guy Peter's article that appears in the *Public Sector Management* and Governance section of the World Bank's website that was submitted December 4, 2000. http://web.worldbank.org/WBSITE/EXTERNAL/TOPICS/EXTPUBLICSECTORANDGOVERNANCE/0,,contentMDK:20134002~pagePK:210058~piPK:210062~theSitePK:286305,00.html

Chapter 4: The rise of the modern welfare state

Comparative analyses of welfare states around the globe can be found in: Rögnvaldur Hannesson, *Debt, Democracy and the Welfare State: Are Modern Democracies Living on Borrowed Time and Money?* (Palgrave Pivot, 2015); and Eric S. Einhorn and John Logue, *Modern Welfare States: Scandinavian Politics and Policy in the Global Age*, 2nd edn (Praeger, 2003).

Contemporary reflections on the topic are addressed in: Christopher Pierson, Francis G. Castles, and Ingela K. Naumann (eds), *The Welfare State Reader*, 3rd edn (Polity, 2013); Jacob S. Hacker, *The Divided Welfare State: The Battle over Public and Private Social Benefits in the United States* (Cambridge University Press, 2002).

In this chapter, we also drew on insights from Stella Z. Theodoulou, *Policy and Politics in Six Nations: A Comparative Perspective on Policy Making* (Prentice Hall, 2002); and Ravi K. Roy and Arthur T. Denzau, *Fiscal Policy Convergence from Reagan to Blair: The Left Veers Right* (Routledge, 2004).

For economic perspectives on the modern welfare state, please consider: Molly C. Michelmore, *Tax and Spend: The Welfare State, Tax Politics, and the Limits of American Liberalism* (University of Pennsylvania Press, 2011); Irwin Garfinkel, Lee Rainwater, and Tim Smeeding, *Wealth and Welfare States: Is America a Laggard or Leader?* (Oxford University Press, 2010); Neil Gilbert and Barbara Gilbert, *The Enabling State: Modern Welfare Capitalism in America* (Oxford University Press, 1989); Gosta Esping-Andersen, *The Three Worlds of Welfare Capitalism* (John Wiley & Sons, 2013); Joseph A. Schumpeter, *Capitalism, Socialism and Democracy* (reprint) (Routledge, 2013); Colin Hay and Daniel Wincott, *The Political Economy of European Welfare Capitalism* (21st Century Europe) (Palgrave Macmillan, 2012); Mark Blyth, *Great Transformations: Economic Ideas and Institutional Change in the Twentieth Century* (Cambridge University Press, 2002); Bo Rothstein, *The Social Democratic State: The Swedish Model and the Bureaucratic Problem of Social Reforms* (University of Pittsburgh Press, 1998); Gregory Luebbert, *Liberalism, Fascism, or Social Democracy: Social Classes and the Political Origins of Regimes in Interwar Europe* (Oxford University Press, 1991).

The quote describing the 'golden age of capitalism' by Robert B. Reich was drawn from the book *Supercapitalism: The Transformation of Business, Democracy, and Everyday Life* (Knopf, 2008), p. 17.

The quote defining the term POSDCORB by Luther Gulick and Lyndall Urwick was drawn directly from their *Papers on the Science of Administration* (Routledge Press, 2004), p. 14.

Our textbox on the Waldo–Simon debate focuses on the discussion over positivist, 'hard science'-based, approaches and normative values-based approaches to the study and practice of public administration. For a more detailed and nuanced explanation of this discussion, as well as further analysis on other important topics that we did not cover, we invite the reader to see Michael M. Harmon's article, 'The Simon/Waldo Debate: A Review and Update', *Public Administration Quarterly*, 12(1) (Winter 1989), pp. 437–51, as well as Mark R. Rutgers' essay entitled 'Theory and Scope of Public Administration: An Introduction to the Study's Epistemology', that appeared as part of the 'Foundations of Public Administration' series featured in a 2010 *Public Administration Review* article (retrieved from: <http://www.aspanet.org/public/aspadocs/par/fpa/fpa-theory-article.pdf>). We also suggest: Herbert Simon, 'Reply to Waldo', *American Political Science Review*, 2 (1952), pp. 494–6 and Dwight Waldo, 'Reply to Simon', *American Political Science Review*, 47 (1953), pp. 500–3.

Box 4 leans in part on insights derived from Michael M. Harmon's article, 'The Simon/Waldo Debate A Review And Update', *Public Administration Quarterly*, 12.1 (Winter 1989), pp. 437–451.

Textbox 4 draws also from Dwight Waldo's book *The Administrative State* (New York: Holmes and Meier, 2nd ed. 1948, 1984), p.171 and his article 'Development Theory of Public Administration', *American Political Science Review*, 46 (1952): 97.

Chapter 5: The New Public Management goes global

Perspectives on the political-economic issues can be found in: Paul Posner, *The Politics of Unfunded Mandates: Whither Federalism?* (Georgetown University Press, 1998); Edward Gramlich, *A Guide to Cost Benefit Analysis*, 2nd edn (Prentice-Hall, 1997); David Osborne and Ted Gaebler, *Reinventing Government: How the Entrepreneurial Spirit is Transforming the Public Sector* (Plume, 1993).

Leadership aspects of public management are highlighted in: Janet Denhardt and Robert Denhardt, *The New Public Service: Serving, Not Steering* (Routledge, 2015); Rosemary O'Leary and Lisa Bingham (eds), *The Collaborative Public Manager: New Ideas for the Twenty-first Century* (Georgetown University Press, 2008); Jan-Erik Lane, *New Public Management: An Introduction* (Routledge, 2002).

For comparative analysis of public management in the United States and abroad, please consider: Siobhan O'Sullivan and Mark Considine, *Contracting-out Welfare Services: Comparing National Policy Designs for Unemployment Assistance* (John Wiley & Sons, 2015); Alison Griffith and Dorothy Smith, *Under New Public Management: Institutional Ethnographies of Changing Front-Line Work* (University of Toronto Press, 2014); Christopher Pollitt and Geert Bouckaert, *Public Management Reform: A Comparative Analysis*, 3rd edn (Oxford University Press, 2011); Ewan Ferlie, Kathleen McLaughlin, and Stephen Osborne (eds), *New Public Management: Current Trends and Future Prospects* (Routledge, 2005).

For an overview on neoliberal governance, please see David Harvey, *A Brief History of Neoliberalism* (Oxford University Press, 2007). The textbox on 'Neoliberalism' and other information from this chapter drew summarily on insights from Manfred B. Steger and Ravi K. Roy, *Neoliberalism: A Very Short Introduction* (Oxford University Press, 2010).

The source for Box 8 is David Osborne and Ted Gaebler, 'Reinventing government (1992)', cited in Robert B. Denhardt, *Theories of Public Organization*, 5th ed. (Wadsworth, 2007).

Chapter 6: The new administrative age

For an excellent discussion on civic engagement, participatory governance, and collaborative management, please see Robert D. Putnam, *Bowling Alone: The Collapse and Revival of American Community* (Touchstone Books by Simon & Schuster, 2001).

We also suggest: Michael McGuire, *Collaborative Public Management: New Strategies for Local Governments* (Georgetown University Press, 2003); and Eugene Bardach, *Getting Agencies to Work Together: The Practice and Theory of Managerial Craftsmanship* (Brookings Institution Press, 1998).

For perspectives on reflective practice and public value, please see Donald A. Schön, *The Reflective Practitioner: How Professionals Think in Action* (Basic Books, 1984); and Mark Moore, *Creating Public Value: Strategic Management in Government* (Harvard University Press, 1995). Relatedly, we also suggest: Terry Cooper, *The Responsible Administrator: An Approach to Ethics for the Administrative Role*, 6th edn (Jossey-Bass, 2012).

For deeper insights on 'systems thinking' and 'profound knowledge', please see W. Edwards Deming, *The New Economics for Industry, Government and Education*, 2nd edn (MIT Press, 2000). For a readable and concise overview of Deming and 'quality management', please see William J. Bellows' three-part article entitled 'Lessons from Deming: A Brief History of Quality' published in the *Lean Management Journal*: 'Part-One', March 2015; 'Part-Two', April 2015; 'Part-Three', May 2015.

The table entitled 'Characteristics of a learning organization' that appears in this chapter was included with the expressed permission of Gipsie B. Ranney.

Box 9 is adapted from The W. Edwards Deming Institute and W. Edwards Deming, *Out of the Crisis* (MIT Press) <https://deming.org/theman/theories/fourteenpoints>.

The source for Box 10 is Robert B. Denhardt, Janet V. Denhardt, and Maria P. Aristigueta, *Managing Human Behavior in Public and Nonprofit Organizations* (Sage Publications, 2012).

Consistent with the scope and accessibility of this *Very Short Introduction*, we have attempted to hold fast to providing a general discussion of various methodological approaches related to the study of public administration. Approaches emphasizing meticulously constructed narratives to explain why public administrators think and behave the way that they do within particular contexts have been gaining traction within the discourse over the last ten years. A growing body of 'interpretivist'-based methodological work emphasizing the ascription of particular meanings, known as 'Hermeneutics', draws inspiration from cultural anthropology. Work in this promising area could be applied to help improve our conceptual precision when studying and analysing various interpretations and meanings pertaining to such terms as 'reflective practice', 'systems thinking', and other values-based 'New Public Service' approaches. For readers seeking to explore 'interpretivist' approaches to public administration and governance in greater depth, we would like to suggest: Colin Hay, 'Interpreting Interpretivism Interpreting Interpretations: The New Hermeneutics of Public Administration', *Public Administration* 89(1) (March 2011), pp. 167–82; and Mark Bevir and R. A. W. Rhodes, *Interpreting British Governance: London* (Routledge, 2003).

Chapter 7: Globalization and the rise of network governance

For a solid analytical overview of globalization and network governance, please see Ali Farazmand, *Public Administration in a Global Context* (Routledge, 2015); Robert Agranoff, *Managing Within Networks: Adding Value to Public Organizations* (Georgetown University Press, 2007); Stephen Goldsmith and William D. Eggers, *Governing by Network: The New Shape of the Public Sector* (Washington, DC: Brookings Institution Press, 2004).

We also suggest: Christopher Reddick, *Public Administration and Information Technology* (Jones & Bartlett Publishers, 2011); Robert Behn, 'The challenge of evaluating m-government, e-government, and p-government: what should be compared with what?', in Viktor Mayer-Schonberger and David Lazer (eds), *Governance in Information Technology: From Electronic Government to Information Government* (MIT Press, 2007), pp. 215–38; Viktor Mayer-Schonberger and David Lazer (eds), *Governance and Information Technology: From Electronic Government to Information Government* (MIT Press, 2007); G. Grant and D. Chau, 'Developing a generic framework for e-Government', in G. Hunter and F. Tan (eds), *Advanced Topics in Global Information Management* (Idea Group, 2006), pp. 72–101; Patrick Dunleavy, Helen Margetts, Simon Bastow, and Jane Tinkler, *Digital Era Governance: IT Corporations, The State, and E-Government* (Oxford University Press, 2006); Darrell West, *Digital Government: Technology and Public Sector Performance* (Princeton University Press, 2005); Jane Fountain,

Building the Virtual State: Information Technology and Institutional Change (Brookings Institution Press, 2001).

The source for Box 11 is Robert Agranoff, *Managing Within Networks: Adding Value to Public Organizations* (Georgetown University Press, 2007).

Chapter 8: The future of public administration

Forward-looking perspectives on public administration can be found in: Carolyn Ban and Norma M. Riccucci (eds), *Public Personnel Management: Current Concerns, Future Challenges*, 2nd edn (Longman, 1997); Mary E. Guy and Marilyn M. Rubin (eds), *Public Administration Evolving: From Foundations to the Future* (Routledge, 2015); Rosemary O'Leary, David Van Slyke, and Soonhee Kim (eds), *The Future of Public Administration Around the World: The Minnowbrook Perspective* (Georgetown University Press, 2011); B. Guy Peters, *The Future of Governing* (University Press of Kansas, 2001); Mark Blyth, *Austerity: The History of a Dangerous Idea* (Oxford University Press, 2013).

The survey data cited from the Ipsos MORI report was drawn from a news release pertaining to a *New Accenture Report*, 22 October 2012. According to the news release, 'Accenture asked Oxford Economics to project total government spending on public service through 2025 in 10 countries—Australia, Brazil, Canada, France, Germany, India, Italy, Singapore, the United Kingdom and the United States'. <https://newsroom.accenture.com/subjects/research-surveys/future-demand-for-public-services-driven-by-an-aging-population-will-cost-the-us-government-an-additional-940-billion-by-2025-according-to-new-accenture-report.htm>.

"牛津通识读本"已出书目

古典哲学的趣味	福柯	地球
人生的意义	缤纷的语言学	记忆
文学理论入门	达达和超现实主义	法律
大众经济学	佛学概论	中国文学
历史之源	维特根斯坦与哲学	托克维尔
设计，无处不在	科学哲学	休谟
生活中的心理学	印度哲学祛魅	分子
政治的历史与边界	克尔凯郭尔	法国大革命
哲学的思与惑	科学革命	民族主义
资本主义	广告	科幻作品
美国总统制	数学	罗素
海德格尔	叔本华	美国政党与选举
我们时代的伦理学	笛卡尔	美国最高法院
卡夫卡是谁	基督教神学	纪录片
考古学的过去与未来	犹太人与犹太教	大萧条与罗斯福新政
天文学简史	现代日本	领导力
社会学的意识	罗兰·巴特	无神论
康德	马基雅维里	罗马共和国
尼采	全球经济史	美国国会
亚里士多德的世界	进化	民主
西方艺术新论	性存在	英格兰文学
全球化面面观	量子理论	现代主义
简明逻辑学	牛顿新传	网络
法哲学：价值与事实	国际移民	自闭症
政治哲学与幸福根基	哈贝马斯	德里达
选择理论	医学伦理	浪漫主义
后殖民主义与世界格局	黑格尔	批判理论

德国文学	儿童心理学	电影
戏剧	时装	俄罗斯文学
腐败	现代拉丁美洲文学	古典文学
医事法	卢梭	大数据
癌症	隐私	洛克
植物	电影音乐	幸福
法语文学	抑郁症	免疫系统
微观经济学	传染病	银行学
湖泊	希腊化时代	景观设计学
拜占庭	知识	神圣罗马帝国
司法心理学	环境伦理学	大流行病
发展	美国革命	亚历山大大帝
农业	元素周期表	气候
特洛伊战争	人口学	第二次世界大战
巴比伦尼亚	社会心理学	中世纪
河流	动物	工业革命
战争与技术	项目管理	传记
品牌学	美学	公共管理